THE SATOSHI STRATEGY

THE SATOSHI STRATEGY

*Bitcoin, System Dynamics, and the
Architecture of Sound Money*

Christopher Battle

Staten Books

2026

First published 2026 by Staten Books

ISBN 979-8-90417-545-0

Typeset in Georgia

Printed by Staten Books

This book does not constitute investment advice. The views expressed are those of the author alone.

Contents

Index127

Introduction

The Book and the Balance Sheet

"I read it and I decided to buy $425 million of bitcoin. The best compliment I can give this book is that it blew my mind."

— Michael Saylor, on The Bitcoin Standard by Saifedean Ammous

Sometime in May 2020, in an office in Tysons Corner, Virginia, Michael Saylor sat down with a book.

He had been reading obsessively for weeks. The pandemic had arrived, the lockdowns had emptied the roads outside his window, and the Federal Reserve had just announced that it would purchase assets in "unlimited" quantities — a word the central bank had never used before, and whose meaning, Saylor had decided, deserved very careful attention. He was fifty-five years old. He had built his company, MicroStrategy, from a basement office in the Virginia suburbs into a NASDAQ-listed enterprise over three decades, survived a catastrophe that had briefly made him the largest single-day loser of personal wealth in recorded history, rebuilt slowly and quietly, and spent twenty years accumulating a cash reserve with the discipline of a man who had once watched everything disappear and had no intention of watching it happen again. He had half a billion dollars sitting in liquid assets. He had, in other words, done everything right.

And now he wasn't so sure.

The book was *The Bitcoin Standard,* by an economist named Saifedean Ammous. It had been published in 2018. Saylor had not read it then. He had not, until recently, taken Bitcoin seriously at all — he had dismissed it publicly as recently as 2013, comparing it to online gambling. But he was working through a reading list now, driven by the same instinct that had always governed his thinking: when something important is changing, find the framework. Don't react to the symptom. Find the structure.

He put the book down some time later and sat very still.

What Ammous had given him was not new information. It was a new lens. The argument ran from the earliest history of money — the seashells and limestone discs, the metals, the coins, the gold standard and its dismemberment — to a proposition that crystallised everything Saylor had been circling for weeks without being able to name: that the monetary system created after Nixon closed the gold window in 1971 was structurally configured, by its own internal logic, to erode the purchasing power of everyone who stored value in it. Not through malice. Not through incompetence. Through structure. The system was working exactly as its architecture dictated. The problem was the architecture.

And Bitcoin, Ammous argued, had been built as the answer. Its supply was fixed at twenty-one million units, enforced not by the promise of any institution but by the consensus rules of a distributed network that no government could override, no central bank could expand, and no political emergency could compromise. It was, in the precise sense, the monetary instrument that the post-1971 system was not: one whose value could not be manufactured at will by the people who controlled it.

Saylor later described what happened when he put the book down with the economy of a man who had made up his mind. "The best compliment I can give this book," he said, "is that I read it and I decided to buy $425 million of bitcoin. It blew my mind."

Three months later, MicroStrategy made its first purchase. By December, the company had committed nearly its entire cash reserve. The financial press was baffled. The short sellers circled. The Wall Street consensus concluded, with the serene confidence of people who had not read the book, that Saylor had lost the plot.

This book is the story of that decision — where it came from, why it was right, and what it means that a man had to read a book in May 2020 to arrive at a conclusion that, in retrospect, seems obvious.

It is not obvious. That is the point. The argument Saylor absorbed from Ammous had been available, in various forms, for more than a century. Ludwig von Mises had made the structural case against fiat monetary expansion in Vienna in 1912. Murray Rothbard had extended it in 1962. The framework was there. The diagnosis was there. What was missing was a technology that could implement the solution — a monetary instrument whose supply constraint was genuinely immune to political override. Bitcoin provided that technology in 2009. Ammous explained why in 2018. Saylor acted in 2020. Between Mises and MicroStrategy lay a hundred and eight years of an argument waiting for the world to catch up.

But the Ammous book is only one of the ingredients. To understand why Saylor's analysis was so precise — why he could look at the post-1971 monetary system and see not just a policy problem but a structural one, not just a bad decision by Nixon but the predictable output of a feedback architecture that had been running without a governor for fifty years — you need to understand something else about how he thinks.

Saylor was trained at MIT in the 1980s in a discipline called System Dynamics. It was founded in the late 1950s by Jay Wright Forrester, an electrical engineer from a Nebraska ranch who had spent his career building feedback systems of extraordinary complexity — servomechanisms, digital computers, the Cold War air-defence network — before concluding that the most important systems in the world were not being designed at all. They were just running, accumulating consequences that nobody was tracking, until the consequences arrived so suddenly and severely that everyone called them a shock. Forrester's foundational claim was that this was not bad luck or bad management. It was structure. Systems behave according to their architecture. Change the people and the behaviour recurs. Change the architecture and the behaviour changes.

Saylor had absorbed this deeply enough as a student to write his undergraduate thesis applying it to the political stability of Renaissance Italian city-states. He had then spent thirty years running a software company, and in the spring of 2020 the framework came back with the force of something long known but not recently needed. The monetary system, seen through the Forrester lens, was not a mystery. It was a control system with a dominant reinforcing loop and a disabled balancing constraint — a system, in other words, that had been structurally configured to expand indefinitely, and would do so until something external stopped it. Fiat currency was not failing. It was succeeding. The problem was what it was designed to do.

There was a third piece, and it came from a different tradition entirely. Marc Andreessen had watched the internet go from academic fringe to civilisational substrate and retained, with unusual precision, the memory of what the dismissal phase looked like. When he published an essay in the New York Times in January 2014 arguing that Bitcoin was structurally comparable to the early internet — an open protocol whose utility compounded with every new participant, generating the self-reinforcing adoption dynamics that eventually make a network impossible to dislodge — he was a decade early, and completely right. The historian Niall Ferguson made the same point in a different register in 2017, arguing in *The Square and the Tower* that the most consequential disruptions in history had always come from distributed horizontal networks that the vertical hierarchies of power could not contain. Bitcoin, designed from its foundations to be a network the tower cannot capture, was another instance of the pattern.

Three frameworks. Three traditions. The monetary economist's diagnosis of the fiat system. The systems engineer's reading of its feedback architecture. The network analyst's understanding of what Bitcoin's adoption dynamics would produce. Saylor held all three simultaneously, in the spring of 2020, reading a book in an office in Virginia while the Federal Reserve announced unlimited asset purchases. The convergence was not planned. Ideas do not arrange themselves by appointment. But when three independent analytical traditions point at the same structure from different angles, it is usually because the structure is real.

What followed was the most consequential corporate treasury decision in recent financial history, and one of the more remarkable examples in modern business of an idea whose time had come finding the mind that could act on it. Saylor did not merely adopt Bitcoin. He became its most visible institutional advocate, giving hundreds of hours of public interviews in which he explained the structural argument in exhausting detail, hosted conferences for corporate treasurers, wrote the foreword to a revised edition of the book that had changed his thinking. He gave the model away. And the adoption wave that followed — sixty-one public companies, nearly a million coins in corporate treasuries, sovereign governments, the world's largest asset manager — is the feedback signal from a structural dynamic that his decision helped to cross a threshold.

This book traces that story from its roots. It begins with a Nebraska ranch and an electrical engineer who realised that the most important unsolved problem in the world was not technical. It moves through the history of the monetary system from Bretton Woods to the pandemic expansion, reading that history through the lens Forrester built. It arrives at Saylor, the book that changed him, and the decision that followed. And it ends by asking what all of it means — for money, for the institutions built on it, and for the question of what kind of knowledge makes the difference between watching a system and understanding it.

Somewhere in that question is why a man had to read a book in May 2020 to see something that had been structurally visible for fifty years.

That is the puzzle this book sets out to solve.

* * *

All quotations from Michael Saylor are drawn from recorded interviews, published transcripts, and his foreword to the revised edition of Saifedean Ammous's The Bitcoin Standard. This book does not constitute investment advice.

Chapter 1
The Engineering Lens

"Structure determines behaviour. If you want to understand the most important problems facing the world, you need to understand the systems that generate those problems."

— Jay Wright Forrester

Michael Saylor does not approach the world as a financier. He approaches it as an engineer.

This distinction is not stylistic. It is structural. It is, in fact, the single most important thing to understand about the man whose corporate treasury decision in August 2020 would eventually redirect tens of billions of dollars into Bitcoin. Because the decision did not emerge from a trading desk, or from a hedge fund's risk model, or from the speculative fever of a bull market. It emerged from a way of seeing the world that Saylor absorbed as an undergraduate at the Massachusetts Institute of Technology in the mid-1980s — a way of seeing that most people have never encountered, and that those who have encountered it have often chosen not to advertise.

That way of seeing has a name. It is called System Dynamics. And if you have never heard of it, that is not an accident.

The Ranch Boy and the Servomechanism

The story of System Dynamics begins not in a laboratory but on a cattle ranch in Nebraska, in the middle of the American Great Plains. Jay Wright Forrester was born there in 1918, into a world without electricity. As a teenager, using nothing more than old automobile parts, he built a wind-driven electrical system that provided his family's ranch with power for the first time. It was a thoroughly practical act of engineering, performed by a boy who had never seen a university, and it established a pattern that would define six decades of intellectual work: start with a real problem, build a system that solves it, and pay close attention to what happens when you turn it on.

Forrester won a scholarship to the University of Nebraska, where he studied electrical engineering — a discipline that, as he would later observe, was "about the only academic field with a solid core of theoretical dynamics." In 1939 he arrived at MIT as a graduate student and was placed under the supervision of Gordon S. Brown in the Servomechanisms Laboratory. It was the beginning of the Second World War, and the problems confronting Brown's laboratory were urgent, mechanical, and deadly.

Aircraft were flying faster than human reaction time could reliably manage. Anti-aircraft gunners could see their targets, but by the time they aimed and fired, the aircraft had moved. The problem was not a lack of intelligence or skill. The problem was delay. In a fast-changing environment, the gap between observation and action was sufficient to render human judgment ineffective. The response was a device called a servomechanism: a closed-loop control system that continuously measured its own deviation from a target and fed that error signal back into its own mechanism. The gun tracked the aircraft not by following orders from a human brain, but by correcting itself, moment by moment, using the difference between where it was pointing and where it needed to point.

For Brown and Forrester, this was not merely a solution to a specific wartime problem. It was a revelation about the architecture of effective action in a world governed by change. A servomechanism replaced discretionary reaction with structural self-correction. Output became input. Correction was embedded in the system, not imposed from outside. Stability was not achieved by adding more supervision. It was achieved by designing the right feedback loop.

This idea — that a system's ability to regulate itself depends on its internal structure rather than on the intelligence of its operators — was the seed from which an entire intellectual tradition would grow.

From Whirlwind to the Sloan School

After the war, Forrester did not return to Nebraska. He stayed at MIT and led one of the most ambitious computing projects of the twentieth century: Project Whirlwind, the construction of one of the first real-time digital computers. Whirlwind was designed to perform calculations fast enough to guide military responses as events unfolded — an engineering challenge that, once again, forced its designers to think about feedback, delay, and the behaviour of systems under stress.

In the course of this work, Forrester invented and patented magnetic-core memory, which became the standard form of computer RAM for roughly two decades. He then became a central figure in the development of SAGE — the Semi-Automatic Ground Environment — a vast Cold War air-defence network that linked radar installations, command centres, and interceptor aircraft across North America. When fully deployed, SAGE connected twenty-seven sites via modems and twenty-five thousand telephone lines. At its heart were enormous IBM computers, each occupying an entire floor of a purpose-built concrete bunker. The system tracked incoming aircraft in real time and computed interception trajectories. It remained operational until 1984.

SAGE was engineering on a civilisational scale, and it taught Forrester something profound about resilient design. The system had to operate under conditions of extreme stress: potential nuclear attack. It could not depend on a single point of control. Every critical function required redundancy. Every node had to be capable of continuing to operate if other nodes were destroyed. Resilience was not achieved by making any single component stronger, but by distributing function across the network so that no single failure could bring the whole down. A robust system degrades gracefully under pressure. It does not shatter.

But the lesson Forrester drew from SAGE went beyond military architecture. He had spent fifteen years building computing systems of extraordinary complexity, and he had come to a conclusion that would redirect his entire career. The biggest impediment to progress, he decided, came not from the engineering side of complex problems, but from the management side. Physical systems, however intricate, could be understood and controlled. Social systems — corporations, cities, economies — could not, because the people running them did not understand the feedback structures that governed their behaviour.

In 1956, at the age of thirty-eight, Forrester made a decision that astonished his engineering colleagues. He left the Department of Electrical Engineering and joined the newly formed MIT Sloan School of Management. He had been, by this point, one of the most decorated engineers of his generation: inventor of core memory, director of Whirlwind, architect of SAGE. He walked away from all of it to study management. His colleagues thought he was mad.

He knew exactly what he was doing.

What followed at Sloan was the creation of not just a new discipline but a new kind of intellectual culture. Forrester ran his group the way he had run engineering teams: hire talented people, give them space, and hold them to punishing standards. Peter Senge, who would later become Forrester's most famous student, arrived as a young master's candidate in 1970 and was hired after a conversation so informal it barely qualified as an interview. Forrester showed him his desk and told him to come back in a month or so to report on how things were going. That was the extent of his supervision.

The freedom was real, but so was the rigour. Senge later recalled the experience of co-drafting a chapter with Forrester on monetary modelling. He would submit a draft; Forrester would return it covered in so much red ink that the underlying text was barely legible. Draft after draft came back looking, in Senge's words, like "bloody battlegrounds." It was through this process that Senge discovered, to his dismay, that he had completed nearly twenty years of formal education without ever learning to write. After months of agony and what felt like an endless succession of rewrites, Forrester offered the only encouragement Senge would ever receive from him. "I too once had to go through this process," Forrester said. "My experience is that you only have to do it once."

Among the members of Forrester's research group, a saying circulated that captured the man perfectly: "He never tells you that you are right. He just stops telling you the ways you are wrong."

Yet there was, beneath this exacting exterior, something subtler and more remarkable. Senge noticed that Forrester was the first professor he had ever encountered who regularly prefaced his comments on a subject with the phrase, "I do not really understand this very deeply." It was a striking admission in a university environment where the prevailing currency was certainty. Years later, a visitor to the group who had spent an afternoon with Forrester made an observation that stayed with Senge for decades: "I have never met a person so able to not know." The visitor continued: "I know much of what I shared with Jay he did not understand, yet this did not seem to bother him in the least. It was like he could just sit and hold each idea, like a rock."

This capacity — the willingness to sit with unresolved contradiction, to hold conflicting data without rushing to premature synthesis — is not common among intellectuals. Senge would later learn, on a hiking trip in the Alps, that a Hungarian physicist who had worked at Niels Bohr's institute in Copenhagen had observed the same quality in Bohr himself. The young physicists around Bohr, brilliant and competitive, had sometimes doubted how sharp the great man really was; he didn't seem to have much energy for intellectual duelling. But, the Hungarian told Senge: "When he understood, he really understood."

Forrester understood. And what he understood, he built.

The Puzzling Factory

Almost immediately upon arriving at Sloan, Forrester was approached by managers from General Electric. They had a problem they could not solve. Their household appliance plants in Kentucky were caught in a punishing three-year cycle: one year the factories would be running seven days a week on three shifts, and two years later half the workforce would be laid off. The cycle repeated with grinding regularity. GE's managers blamed the business cycle. External demand must be fluctuating. Customers were fickle. Markets were unpredictable.

Forrester was not persuaded. He sat down with a pencil and a notebook. At the top of the page, he drew columns for inventories, employees, orders, and production rates. Then, working forward week by week, he traced how each variable would change in response to the others, given the decision rules that GE's own managers were using. When orders rose, managers hired workers. Hiring took time. While waiting for the new workers to arrive, backlogs grew. Seeing the backlogs, managers placed even more orders for materials. When the new workers finally arrived, production surged. Inventories overshot. Orders dried up. Managers laid off workers. The cycle began again.

The insight was devastating in its simplicity. Even if incoming customer orders had remained perfectly constant — never fluctuating at all — the factory would still have oscillated. The instability was not caused by the external environment. It was caused by the internal structure of the firm's own decision-making process. Specifically, it was caused by the interaction of feedback loops, accumulations, and time delays within a system whose operators did not understand they were part of one.

This was the founding insight of System Dynamics: behaviour is produced by structure. If a system behaves in a particular way repeatedly, the explanation lies not in the personalities operating it, nor in the external shocks impinging upon it, but in the architecture governing it. Change the people and the behaviour will recur. Change the structure and the behaviour will change.

Forrester published this analysis in 1961 as *Industrial Dynamics*, the first book in the field. The phenomenon he identified — that small perturbations in consumer demand are amplified into large swings in production as they propagate up a supply chain — became known as the Forrester effect, and later as the bullwhip effect. It remains one of the most important discoveries in operations management. And it was produced by a man sitting in a room with a pencil, thinking about what happens when decision-makers respond to visible symptoms without understanding the delayed consequences of their own responses.

Stocks, Flows, and the Logic of Accumulation

From this founding case, Forrester developed a formal language for analysing the dynamic behaviour of any system that changes over time. The language is built on two elementary concepts: stocks and flows.

A stock is an accumulation. It is a quantity that changes only gradually, over time. The water in a bathtub is a stock. The money in a bank account is a stock. The inventory in a warehouse, the carbon dioxide in the atmosphere, the national debt, the number of Bitcoin held in a corporate treasury — each of these is a stock. It can be measured at any moment, and its level at any given moment is the result of everything that has flowed into it and out of it over its entire history.

A flow is a rate of change. It is the process that increases or decreases a stock. The water pouring from the tap is an inflow.

The water draining from the plug is an outflow. The rate of hiring is an inflow to a workforce stock. The rate of attrition is an outflow. Flows are measured per unit of time: litres per minute, employees per month, tonnes of carbon per year.

This distinction seems almost trivially simple. It is not. Human intuition, as decades of subsequent experimental research would demonstrate, is catastrophically bad at reasoning about stocks and flows. We focus on flows because they are visible and immediate. We underweight stocks because they change slowly and are easy to ignore. And we persistently fail to grasp the most important consequence of the stock-flow relationship: that when you change a flow, the effect on the stock is delayed. The stock does not respond instantly. It accumulates. And by the time the accumulation becomes visible, the original cause may have been forgotten.

Consider the bathtub. If the tap is running faster than the drain is emptying, the water level rises. Everyone understands this. But if you ask people — even highly educated people — to reason about a system with exactly this structure in an unfamiliar context, most of them get it wrong. John Sterman, Forrester's intellectual heir at MIT and the current director of the System Dynamics Group, demonstrated this with a series of elegant experiments. He gave graduate students at MIT — students with degrees in science, technology, engineering, and economics — a non-technical description of the global carbon cycle, including the fact that humanity is currently emitting carbon dioxide into the atmosphere at roughly twice the rate at which natural processes remove it. He then asked them to sketch, on a simple graph, what would need to happen to emissions in order to stabilise atmospheric CO_2 concentrations by the year 2100.

The results were alarming. Eighty-four per cent of participants drew trajectories that violated the most basic principles of accumulation. Most sketched emissions paths in which emissions stopped growing but remained above the rate of removal — the equivalent of claiming that a bathtub continuously filled faster than it drains will never overflow.

Nearly two-thirds asserted that atmospheric greenhouse gases could stabilise even while emissions continuously exceeded removal. These were not members of the public. They were MIT graduate students. And they could not reason correctly about a bathtub.

This is not a curiosity. It is a structural feature of human cognition that has consequences for every domain in which accumulation, delay, and feedback interact — which is to say, for virtually every important domain of human affairs. Monetary policy. Fiscal debt. Corporate balance sheets. Epidemiology. Climate. And, as Michael Saylor would eventually perceive with unusual clarity, the long-run behaviour of reserve assets in a world of elastic monetary supply.

The Beer Game

If there is a single artifact that captures the spirit of System Dynamics — its method, its mischief, and its moral — it is the Beer Game.

The Beer Game is not a computer simulation. It is a table game, played with pen, paper, printed plastic tablecloths, and poker chips. It was created by Forrester in the late 1950s, originally as the "Refrigerator Game" (after the GE appliance problem that inspired it), and was later renamed and refined. Since 1998, John Sterman has run it every year at MIT Sloan's new-student orientation, presiding over a scene of controlled chaos in a Cambridge hotel ballroom.

Picture the room. Four hundred incoming MBA students from forty-one countries file in on a humid August afternoon. They sit down in teams of eight at forty-seven tables, each covered with a long vinyl game board. Each player occupies a position in a simulated beer supply chain: retailer, wholesaler, distributor, or brewery. Customer demand is represented by cards turned over at one end. Poker chips represent cases of beer. Each player's job is simple: keep your customers supplied while minimising your costs, which accrue from both holding excess inventory and running short.

There is one critical constraint. Players cannot communicate with each other. The retailer sees customer demand but the wholesaler does not. The wholesaler sees the retailer's orders but not the end-customer's demand. The only information each player has is the orders arriving from the position immediately downstream and the deliveries arriving from the position immediately upstream. Everyone is trying to do a sensible job. No one is irrational. No one is cheating.

Within twenty minutes, the room descends into pandemonium. Students are shouting, gesturing, laughing, and swearing. Backlogs explode. Inventories rocket to absurd levels. One year, the worst-performing team accumulated costs of $6,618 against a theoretical optimum of roughly $200. The distributor on the losing team went from a backlog of seventy cases to an inventory surplus of one hundred and ninety-one in the space of three simulated weeks.

What happened? The customer demand, which the players were not told, had increased by a single step early in the game — a small, one-time increase — and then remained flat. That was the only external shock. Everything else that happened — the wild swings, the shortages, the towering surpluses, the panic — was generated internally, by the interaction of the players' own ordering decisions with the delays built into the supply chain.

When Sterman debriefs the game, he begins with a question: what caused the oscillations? Almost universally, the players blame each other. The retailer blames the wholesaler for not shipping fast enough. The wholesaler blames the distributor. The distributor blames the brewery. Everyone blames the customer for volatile demand. This is the most natural thing in the world. It is also completely wrong.

The demand was stable. The system was unstable. And the instability was generated by the structure of the supply chain interacting with the decision rules of its participants. Each player, seeing a shortage, responded by ordering more. But their orders took time to arrive. While they waited, the shortage continued, so they ordered even more. By the time the original order arrived, demand had stabilised and inventory piled up.

Each person, acting individually, was doing something that appeared reasonable. Collectively, they produced catastrophe.

In his landmark 1989 paper in *Management Science*, Sterman proposed a formal model of the decision-making heuristic that players use in the Beer Game. He called it the "anchoring and adjustment" model and identified several specific "misperceptions of feedback" that account for the poor performance. Players were insensitive to the feedback from their own decisions to their environment. They ignored the supply line of orders already placed but not yet received. They confused flow rates with stock levels. They reacted to symptoms rather than to the structural causes of those symptoms.

This was Forrester's GE insight replicated under controlled conditions: intelligent, well-intentioned managers, given identical information and identical incentive structures, systematically produce oscillation, overshoot, and instability. The problem is not the people. It is the interaction between the people's mental models and the structure of the system they inhabit.

The Beer Game has now been played tens of thousands of times, in universities, corporations, and government agencies around the world. The results are invariant. Regardless of nationality, industry experience, or educational background, the pattern repeats. As Sterman put it, the game demonstrates that "the internal structure of a system is more important than external events in generating the behaviour we observe."

This is the foundational proposition of System Dynamics, reduced to an afternoon's poker chips and vinyl tablecloths: *structure determines behaviour.*

Policy Resistance: Why Good Intentions Fail

The Beer Game illustrates a specific form of a broader phenomenon that System Dynamics calls policy resistance. A system resists correction because the correction fails to account for accumulated momentum, delayed effects, and the feedback responses that the correction itself provokes.

Forrester encountered this pattern everywhere he looked. When he turned his attention to urban planning in the late 1960s, collaborating with John Collins, the former mayor of Boston who happened to occupy the office next door, the results were profoundly counterintuitive. The *Urban Dynamics* model, published in 1969, showed that constructing low-income housing in struggling urban areas — the most intuitively compassionate policy response — actually deepened poverty. How? The housing attracted population but did not attract employment. Land that might have supported job-creating enterprises was consumed by residential construction. The ratio of people to jobs worsened. Conditions deteriorated further. The politically attractive solution made the problem worse.

The politically unattractive solution — demolishing old housing to free land for commercial development — generated employment, improved the tax base, and over time raised living standards. This was not a finding calculated to endear Forrester to city councils. As he later recalled, audiences for his urban dynamics presentations would "become more and more negative and emotional" as they worked through the model's logic. But Forrester also told a revealing story: a journalist, having attended one of these sessions, later visited a man in New York who had been briefed on the work two years earlier. The man told the journalist: "They don't just have a solution to the urban problem up there in Boston. They have the only solution." The five hours of exposure to urban dynamics had left a lasting impression, undimmed by time.

Policy resistance occurs in every domain where feedback and delay are present — which is to say, in every important domain of collective human action. Today's problems come from yesterday's solutions, as Peter Senge would later put it. The harder you push, the harder the system pushes back. Behaviour grows better before it grows worse. The easy way out usually leads back in.

These are not slogans. They are structural consequences of feedback, accumulation, and delay. And they are invisible to anyone who has not been trained to look for them.

Distributed Resilience

Alongside feedback and accumulation, Forrester's career contributed a third principle to the System Dynamics framework: distributed resilience.

The lesson came from SAGE. Systems designed to operate under extreme stress could not depend on a single point of control. The network had to be architected so that the failure of any individual node — or even the destruction of several nodes in a nuclear strike — would degrade performance without collapsing the whole. Every critical function had to exist in more than one place. Every pathway had to have an alternative. The system had to be designed, in military parlance, to survive.

This is an architectural principle, not a policy recommendation. A centralised system is efficient under normal conditions but brittle under stress. A distributed system is less efficient in peacetime but vastly more resilient when things go wrong. The choice between centralisation and distribution is a choice about what kind of failure mode you are willing to accept.

For an engineer trained at MIT in the era of SAGE, the analogy to monetary and economic systems is not a metaphor. It is a direct structural comparison. A monetary system with a single point of control — a central bank with discretionary authority over money supply — is a centralised architecture. It may function smoothly under normal conditions. But it is structurally vulnerable to the same pathology as any centralised system: if the controlling node makes errors, there is no redundancy, no failsafe, and no self-correcting mechanism that operates independently of the controller's judgment.

We shall return to this comparison in later chapters. For now, it is sufficient to register the principle: resilient systems distribute control and constrain failure. Fragile systems concentrate control and amplify it.

The Fifth Discipline and the Curious Non-Revolution

By the early 1990s, the intellectual framework that Forrester had built over three decades was more powerful than ever. The computational tools had matured. The DYNAMO programming language, originally written in 1959 by Phyllis Fox and Alexander Pugh, had been succeeded by user-friendly graphical software like STELLA, Vensim, and Powersim. A generation of doctoral students, trained directly by Forrester and Sterman, had applied System Dynamics to problems as varied as corporate strategy, drug policy, the dynamics of the Cold War arms race, and the long-wave economic cycle.

And then something extraordinary happened: System Dynamics almost became famous.

In 1990, Peter Senge, a senior lecturer at MIT who had studied under Forrester, published *The Fifth Discipline: The Art and Practice of the Learning Organization*. The book argued that systems thinking — the ability to see feedback loops, delays, and structural causation rather than isolated events — was the essential discipline for organisations that wished to learn, adapt, and survive. Senge packaged the core insights of System Dynamics in an accessible, almost literary style. He used the Beer Game as a centrepiece. He coined the phrase "learning organisation" and articulated eleven "laws of the fifth discipline" that read like proverbs for the systems age: *today's problems come from yesterday's solutions; the harder you push, the harder the system pushes back; behaviour grows better before it grows worse; the easy way out usually leads back in.*

The book sold over a million copies. The *Harvard Business Review* called it one of the seminal management books of the past seventy-five years. Dr. W. Edwards Deming, the father of Total Quality Management, said he had learned much from it. For a brief, shining moment, it appeared that the most powerful analytical framework produced at MIT in the second half of the twentieth century was about to reshape how the world's organisations were managed.

It didn't.

The *Fifth Discipline* became a bestseller. Systems thinking became a buzzword. The phrase "learning organisation" entered the lexicon of every management consultant. But the hard core of System Dynamics — the formal modelling, the computer simulation, the rigorous stock-flow analysis that gives the framework its actual power — was quietly left behind. Consultants adopted the language. They drew causal loop diagrams on whiteboards. They spoke of "feedback" and "leverage points". But almost none of them built models. Almost none of them ran simulations. Almost none of them did the mathematics.

The result was a peculiar bifurcation. System Dynamics remained extraordinarily influential within its own community — a global network of researchers, a dedicated journal (*System Dynamics Review*), an annual international conference, and a constellation of software tools. Sterman's *Business Dynamics: Systems Thinking and Modeling for a Complex World*, published in 2000, became the definitive textbook, nearly a thousand pages of rigorous exposition. But in the world of mainstream management consulting — at McKinsey, at BCG, at Bain — System Dynamics never became a standard tool. It was acknowledged, occasionally cited, but rarely practised. McKinsey itself republished Forrester's foundational 1995 article. Yet its own consultants did not, for the most part, build System Dynamics models for their clients.

Why? This is one of the great puzzles of twentieth-century intellectual history, and the answer tells us something important about the nature of powerful knowledge.

Forrester himself offered a clue in one of his conversations with Senge. The world of linear analysis — the world in which most engineers, economists, and managers are trained — was, he said, like living inside a tent. "Every once in a while, someone pokes a hole in the tent and gazes at the nonlinear world outside. They then become terrified and quickly go back inside." System Dynamics is, in essence, the discipline of leaving the tent. Its models are nonlinear. Its conclusions are counterintuitive. Its implications are disturbing. Most people, confronted with its findings, experience not enlightenment but vertigo.

Part of the explanation is therefore technical. System Dynamics requires genuine mathematical modelling. It requires building computer simulations, calibrating them against data, running sensitivity analyses, and interpreting nonlinear behaviour. This is hard. It is time-consuming. And it does not lend itself to the production of polished slide decks on a two-week consulting engagement.

Part of the explanation is cultural. The conclusions of System Dynamics models are frequently counterintuitive. They tell clients that their preferred policies will make things worse. They reveal that the "obvious" solution is part of the problem. This is not what clients want to hear, and it is not what consultants are rewarded for telling them. Forrester himself recognised this early. In his 1989 speech to the System Dynamics Society — later republished by McKinsey — he observed that early system dynamics analyses operated in a "consultant mode": the practitioner would study a corporation, go away, build a model, and return with recommendations. "In most cases," he noted, "these suggestions would be accepted as sound, but they would not alter behaviour. Under the pressure of day-to-day operations, decisions would revert to prior practice."

But there is a third explanation, less discussed but perhaps more significant. Some of those who truly understood System Dynamics — who had mastered the modelling, who had seen its predictive power, who had experienced the competitive advantage it conferred — had no particular incentive to popularise it. A tool that reveals counterintuitive truths about complex systems is, almost by definition, more valuable to those who possess it if others do not. If your competitors are trapped in linear thinking, reacting to symptoms, chasing the visible while ignoring the structural, why would you teach them to see?

Forrester himself hinted at this. He observed that system dynamics had "always surprised" him in its public reception, and that he had "usually been wrong in anticipating the impact" his books would make. *World Dynamics*, he noted wryly, "seemed to have everything necessary to guarantee no public notice: forty pages of equations in the middle of the book, key messages in the form of computer output graphs, and a publisher that had only published technical books." Yet it became a global sensation. The popular version, *The Limits to Growth*, sold thirty million copies. The more technical the work, the less it penetrated. The more accessible the packaging, the more the essential difficulty was lost.

System Dynamics thus occupies a peculiar position in the intellectual landscape. It is simultaneously one of the most powerful analytical frameworks ever developed and one of the least widely practised. It has been publicly available since 1961. Its textbooks are in print. Its software is free. And yet the number of people in the world who can actually build and interpret a System Dynamics model of any real complexity remains vanishingly small relative to the number of people who make decisions that could benefit from one.

Whether this is a failure of diffusion or a successful act of intellectual hoarding is a question worth holding in mind as this story unfolds.

Sterman's Inheritance

If Forrester was the founder, John Sterman has been the cathedral builder.

Sterman arrived at MIT in the 1970s and became Forrester's student, colleague, and eventually successor as director of the System Dynamics Group. Where Forrester's instinct was that of the engineer — build the model, present the results, let the logic speak — Sterman added a deep engagement with the psychology of human decision-making. His research programme has been devoted to understanding why intelligent people persistently fail to manage the systems they inhabit.

His answer, developed across dozens of papers and experiments, centres on the concept of "misperceptions of feedback." Sterman has demonstrated, with experimental rigour, that human beings are systematically unable to reason correctly about systems involving feedback, accumulation, and delay. We confuse stocks with flows. We ignore supply lines. We attribute to external causes what is in fact the product of our own decisions interacting with the structure of our environment. We track correlation where we should track accumulation. We see patterns in flows and assume the stock must follow the same pattern — a fallacy as elementary as assuming that a bathtub will stop filling because you've turned down (but not turned off) the tap.

These are not minor errors at the margins of decision-making. They are fundamental cognitive biases that operate at every level of human organisation, from the individual to the civilisational. And they are not corrected by intelligence, education, or experience. The MIT graduate students who could not reason correctly about the carbon bathtub were among the most technically accomplished young people on the planet. They failed not because they were stupid, but because the human brain was not evolved to think in stocks and flows.

Sterman's contribution has been to systematise this insight and to develop tools — what he calls "management flight simulators" — that allow people to experience, in compressed time, the consequences of their own decision-making in dynamic systems. The Beer Game is the most famous, but there are others: simulations of airline management, of technology adoption, of epidemic dynamics. The principle is the same in each: place people inside a system, let them make decisions, and then show them what their decisions actually produced.

The purpose is not to humiliate. It is to teach. As Sterman has observed, "system dynamics is not a spectator sport." You cannot learn it by reading about it. You have to experience the failure of your own intuition in a system whose structure you subsequently come to understand. The gap between what you thought would happen and what actually happened is the space in which learning occurs.

The Lens

Taken together, the intellectual tradition that runs from Gordon Brown's Servomechanisms Laboratory through Forrester's

Industrial Dynamics through Sterman's experimental programme yields a coherent set of propositions about the way the world works:

Structure determines behaviour. If a system produces a persistent pattern, the cause lies in its architecture, not in external events or individual failures.

Feedback governs stability. Systems regulate themselves through loops that either reinforce change (positive feedback) or counteract it (negative feedback). The balance between the two determines whether the system converges, oscillates, or explodes.

Accumulation delays consequence. Because stocks integrate flows over time, the effects of today's decisions may not become visible for months or years. When the consequences finally arrive, they appear abrupt, though they are the product of slow accumulation.

Intuition fails in the presence of dynamic complexity. Human beings are systematically unable to reason correctly about systems involving feedback, accumulation, and delay. Our mental models are linear in a world that is not.

Discretionary intervention can amplify instability. Well-intentioned policies, applied without understanding the system's structure, frequently worsen the problems they aim to solve.

Resilient systems distribute control and constrain failure. Centralised architectures are efficient but brittle. Distributed architectures are less efficient but survivable.

This is the lens through which Michael Saylor sees the world. He did not acquire it from a finance textbook or a trading floor. He acquired it at MIT, in the same intellectual tradition that built servomechanisms, Whirlwind, SAGE, and the Beer Game. He learned to think in stocks and flows, feedback and delay, structure and behaviour.

The Machiavelli Thesis

The evidence that this training was more than superficial lies in Saylor's undergraduate thesis. In 1987, while completing dual degrees in aeronautics and astronautics and in the history of science, technology, and society, Saylor wrote a thesis entitled "A Mathematical Model of a Renaissance Italian City State." It was supervised through the Sloan School's System Dynamics programme.

The thesis applied the tools of System Dynamics to the political theory of Niccolò Machiavelli. Saylor built a computer simulation of a Renaissance Italian city-state with three branches of government and modelled how different forms of government responded to exogenous shocks: war, famine, natural disaster. The simulation examined how institutional structure — not the quality of individual leaders — determined long-term political stability.

This was not a trivial exercise. It demonstrated that the young Saylor had absorbed the deepest lesson of System Dynamics: that the principles governing feedback and structure operate regardless of domain. A servomechanism corrects an anti-aircraft gun. A supply chain oscillates because of its internal ordering rules. A Renaissance city-state rises or falls according to the feedback loops embedded in its political architecture. The same analytical tools apply to all three, because all three are systems governed by stocks, flows, feedback, and delay.

After graduating with the highest honours, Saylor was commissioned as a Second Lieutenant in the United States Air Force but was prevented from entering the jet-pilot programme by a benign heart murmur. Instead, he entered consulting, building computer simulations for companies like DuPont, Dow, and Exxon. In 1989, at the age of twenty-four, he founded MicroStrategy, a business intelligence company that would make him, briefly, one of the richest men in the world.

For the next three decades, he ran his company. He survived a dot-com crash, an SEC investigation, and the slow erosion of his legacy software business. He accumulated cash. He watched. And then, in the spring of 2020, the world changed — and the engineer in him recognised what the change meant.

But that is a story for a later chapter. To understand the decision that would redefine his company and his reputation, we must first understand how the System Dynamics framework applies not merely to factories and supply chains, but to civilisation itself — and what happens when the measuring instrument of the entire global economy begins to malfunction.

An engineer trained in feedback and delay asks a different question from a financier. The financier asks: is the price going up or down? The engineer asks: what is the structure of this system, and what behaviour will that structure produce over time?

The financier watches the flow.

The engineer watches the stock.

* * *

Chapter 2

When Models Meet Reality

"We were at MIT. We had been trained in science. The way we thought about the future was utterly logical: if you tell people there's a disaster ahead, they will change course. If you give them a choice between a good future and a bad one, they will pick the good. They might even be grateful. Naive, weren't we?"

— Donella Meadows

On the evening of 29 June 1970, Jay Forrester boarded a flight from Bern, Switzerland, back to Cambridge, Massachusetts. He had just attended a meeting of the Club of Rome, an informal assembly of about seventy-five European scientists, industrialists, and civil servants who had convened around a question they called the "predicament of mankind": what happens when exponential economic and population growth collides with a finite planet?

The meeting had been frustrating. For two days, the assembled luminaries had talked in circles. They knew the problem was large. They knew its elements were interconnected. They did not have a method for thinking about those interconnections rigorously. They had sophisticated intuitions but no analytical engine.

Forrester had one. On the flight home, he pulled out a sheet of paper and began to sketch.

What he drew was a System Dynamics model of the entire world. Five stocks: population, industrial capital, agricultural capital, natural resources, and pollution. A lattice of feedback loops connecting them. Reinforcing loops that drove growth. Balancing loops that imposed constraint. Delays that separated cause from visible effect. He called it WORLD1. By the time the plane touched down in Massachusetts, he had the skeleton of a model that would, within two years, become the most controversial piece of applied social science of the twentieth century.

That model would sell thirty million copies in its popularised form. It would be denounced by economists, celebrated by environmentalists, and debated in every parliament and lecture hall on earth. It would be proved more right than wrong over the following half-century, though almost nobody at the time believed it. And for the purposes of this book, it would reveal something that its creators never quite intended: the decisive importance of the instrument with which a civilisation measures its own condition.

The Italian and the Engineer

The Club of Rome was the creation of Aurelio Peccei, an Italian industrialist with a remarkable biography. Born in Turin in 1908, Peccei had worked for Fiat, been arrested by Mussolini's fascists in 1944, been imprisoned and tortured, nearly executed, and then escaped to join the resistance. After the war, he helped rebuild Italian industry and eventually became managing director of Olivetti. By the late 1960s, he was consumed by a question that most of his fellow industrialists preferred not to contemplate: what were the long-term consequences of the industrial system that men like him had spent their careers building?

Peccei assembled his Club in 1968, the same year that student protests convulsed Paris and Chicago, and that the Apollo 8 astronauts took the first photograph of Earth from space — the famous "blue marble" image that showed, for the first time, a small and apparently fragile sphere suspended in infinite blackness. It was an era in which the Cuyahoga River in

Ohio had caught fire from the volume of pollutants floating on its surface, in which Rachel Carson's *Silent Spring* had already sounded the alarm about pesticide accumulation in the food chain, and in which the first Earth Day, in April 1970, had drawn twenty million Americans into the streets.

Peccei wanted rigour, not protest. He wanted a method. At the Bern meeting, Forrester offered him one. He told the assembled members of the Club that System Dynamics could model the interactions they were worried about — not as isolated trends, but as a coupled system of stocks, flows, and feedback loops, computed on a digital machine. A fortnight later, a delegation from the Club visited Forrester at MIT, and he demonstrated WORLD2, a refined version of his in-flight sketch. They were convinced.

Forrester chose not to lead the full study himself. He was committed to his ongoing research on urban dynamics, and he preferred to let younger hands take the work forward. Instead, he assembled a team of seventeen researchers, headed by his former doctoral student Dennis Meadows. Meadows was twenty-eight years old. His wife, Donella — known universally as Dana — was a biophysicist with an exceptional talent for clear writing. The Norwegian management scholar Jørgen Randers and the young systems analyst William Behrens III completed the core authoring team. The Volkswagen Foundation provided the funding.

Over the following eighteen months, the team constructed WORLD3, a substantially more elaborate model than Forrester's original sketch. WORLD3 tracked the interactions between five principal variables: world population, industrial production, food production, consumption of non-renewable resources, and pollution. It was written in DYNAMO, the programming language that Phyllis Fox and Alexander Pugh had developed at MIT in 1959 specifically for System Dynamics modelling. The model's equations filled an entire companion volume, *Dynamics of Growth in a Finite World*, a dense technical annex that almost nobody outside the System Dynamics community ever read.

What the world read instead was a slim, accessibly written summary: *The Limits to Growth*.

The Book That Shook the World

The findings were presented at international gatherings in Moscow and Rio de Janeiro in the summer of 1971, and the book was published in February 1972. Its central argument was stark. If prevailing rates of population growth, industrialisation, resource consumption, and pollution generation continued unchanged, the global system would overshoot its carrying capacity and undergo a sharp, uncontrolled decline in both population and industrial output sometime in the mid-twenty-first century.

The mechanism was structural, not speculative. Exponential growth in population and industrial capital increased the rate at which non-renewable resources were extracted. As resources depleted, more and more capital had to be devoted to obtaining them, leaving less available for investment in growth. Eventually, investment could not keep pace with depreciation. The industrial base collapsed, dragging agricultural and service systems down with it, because they had become dependent on industrial inputs — fertilisers, pesticides, energy, hospital equipment, transport. Population, having overshot the carrying capacity that the industrial system had temporarily expanded, fell sharply.

The model did not predict a date. Its creators were careful to say that the graphs were not forecasts but illustrations of "behavioural tendencies." Under twelve different scenarios, varying assumptions about technology, resource discovery, and policy intervention, only four avoided the overshoot-and-collapse pattern. Those four required simultaneous stabilisation of population and industrial output, combined with aggressive recycling and pollution control. In other words, the only path to stability was deliberate constraint.

The Limits to Growth sold twelve million copies in thirty-seven languages. It remains the best-selling environmental book ever published. It landed in the public consciousness at exactly the right moment: the oil shocks of 1973 were just around the corner, and the industrial world was about to discover, painfully, what it meant to depend on a finite resource controlled by others.

The Population Bomb and the Confusion That Followed

To understand what happened next, and why it matters for the argument of this book, it is necessary to disentangle a confusion that has persisted for half a century.

The Limits to Growth was not the only alarm ringing in the early 1970s. Four years before the Club of Rome's project began, in 1968, Paul Ehrlich, a Stanford biologist whose primary expertise was in butterflies, published *The Population Bomb*. Written in a few weeks at the suggestion of David Brower of the Sierra Club, the book opened with one of the most arresting sentences in the history of popular science: "The battle to feed all of humanity is over. In the 1970s and 1980s hundreds of millions of people will starve to death."

Ehrlich became a celebrity. He appeared on Johnny Carson's *Tonight Show* more than twenty times — an astonishing platform for a lepidopterist — and his organisation, Zero Population Growth, swelled from six chapters and six hundred members to six hundred chapters and sixty thousand members. His message was vivid, personal, and terrifying: there were too many people, and unless population was brought under control by whatever means necessary, including, he suggested, compulsory sterilisation and additives in the water supply, civilisation would collapse.

The problem was that Ehrlich made specific, dated predictions, and those predictions were wrong. The hundreds of millions did not starve in the 1970s and 1980s. The Green Revolution — the suite of agricultural innovations in high-yield crop varieties, synthetic fertilisers, and irrigation — dramatically increased food production across Asia and Latin America.

Population growth rates began to decline as development, education, and access to contraception spread. Ehrlich had wagered on a straight-line extrapolation of a single variable — population — and the world had responded with the very innovation and adaptation that straight-line extrapolations cannot capture. As the economist Noah Smith later put it, Ehrlich's method was "really just drawing exponential curves and then saying 'See, line go up!'" It ignored every countermeasure, every adaptation, every feedback response that a population of seven billion ingenious primates would inevitably produce when confronted with a visible threat.

The irony is savage. System Dynamics was built precisely to capture what Ehrlich's method excluded: the feedback loops, the balancing forces, the nonlinear responses that arise endogenously within a system under stress. Ehrlich made the elementary error that Forrester had spent his career diagnosing — the error of extrapolating a single flow while ignoring the stocks, the feedbacks, and the delays that govern the system's actual trajectory. He was, in effect, the kind of thinker that System Dynamics existed to correct.

But Ehrlich was on television. He was charismatic, quotable, and frightening. The MIT team, by contrast, published dense technical models accompanied by computer-generated graphs. Ehrlich predicted that sixty-five million Americans would starve to death in the 1980s and that England would cease to exist by the year 2000. The Meadows team said, carefully, that their graphs were not predictions but illustrations of "behavioural tendencies." One message sold twelve million copies. The other sold two million. Both were filed in the same mental drawer by a public that did not distinguish between a polemic and a model.

The debacle culminated in 1980 in a famous wager. The economist Julian Simon, an ebullient optimist who regarded resource scarcity as a myth corrected by price signals and human ingenuity, challenged Ehrlich to a bet. Ehrlich could choose any five commodity metals; if their inflation-adjusted prices rose over the following decade, Simon would pay the difference. If they fell, Ehrlich would pay. Ehrlich selected copper, chromium, nickel, tin, and tungsten. By September 1990, the price of every one of the five had fallen. Ehrlich posted Simon a cheque for $576.07. It was one of the most public humiliations in the history of the academy, and it was devastating not only to Ehrlich personally but to the broader intellectual project with which he had become entangled.

Here is the confusion that matters. In the public mind, Ehrlich and the *Limits to Growth* became fused into a single narrative: alarmists predicted doom, doom did not arrive, therefore limits do not exist. The debunking of Ehrlich became, by association, a debunking of the MIT team. Simon's victory over Ehrlich became, in the popular imagination, a refutation of System Dynamics.

This was a profound misreading. Ehrlich was not a systems dynamicist. He did not build feedback models. He did not run simulations. He made linear extrapolations from a single variable — population — and predicted specific dated outcomes that depended on those extrapolations holding. His method was the precise opposite of what Forrester and the Meadows team were doing. *The Limits to Growth* did not predict famine by 1985. It did not predict any specific event at any specific date. It said that the *structural tendency* of a system characterised by exponential growth, finite stocks, and delayed feedback was overshoot and collapse — and that the timing would depend on assumptions about technology, policy, and behaviour that the model itself could test under different scenarios.

Ehrlich's *Population Bomb* was a polemic driven by a single obsession. The Meadows team's *Limits to Growth* was a formal model driven by structural analysis. The polemic was falsified. The model, as subsequent data has consistently shown, was not. Yet the reputational damage was done. By the time Simon collected his cheque, the phrase "limits to growth" had become, in the minds of most economists and policymakers, a synonym for discredited alarmism. It was, as Dana Meadows later reflected with weary precision, "naive" to think that the distinction would survive contact with public discourse.

There is a deeper irony in the Simon-Ehrlich bet that neither participant seems to have noticed. Simon's wager was denominated in dollars — inflation-adjusted dollars. The adjustment was necessary because the dollar itself was losing value, and had been losing value at an accelerating rate since 1971, when the gold constraint on its issuance was removed. Simon won his bet in part because commodity prices, measured in constantly depreciating dollars, are a noisy signal that reflects monetary conditions as much as physical scarcity. Had the bet been denominated in a unit of constant purchasing power — in gold, for instance, or in hours of labour required to purchase the metals — the outcome would have been less clear-cut.

Neither the Malthusians nor the cornucopians asked the question that a control engineer would have asked first: is the ruler you are using to measure the outcome itself changing length? We shall return to this question. For now, it is enough to note that the conflation of Ehrlich with the *Limits* team poisoned the well for a generation, and made it nearly impossible for System Dynamics' structural insights to receive a fair hearing in mainstream economics.

The Fury of the Economists

The backlash was ferocious.

Economists, in particular, attacked the model with a vehemence that revealed something beyond mere scholarly disagreement. Three economists writing in the *New York Times Book Review* in 1972 dismissed it as an "empty and misleading work." Henry Wallich, the distinguished Yale economist who would later join the Board of Governors of the Federal Reserve, called its conclusions "nonsense." The *Economist, Newsweek*, and a succession of academic reviewers piled on. The book was characterised as neo-Malthusian, technophobic, and dangerously anti-growth.

The criticism was not without substance. The model treated resources as a single aggregate stock rather than distinguishing between specific commodities with different substitution possibilities. It used static coefficients where dynamic adjustment might have been more appropriate. It assumed that technology would continue along existing trajectories rather than modelling the possibility of disruptive innovation. And the popularised version — Dana Meadows's brilliantly readable summary — inevitably simplified nuances that were present in the technical model.

But the most revealing feature of the criticism was what it did not address. Almost none of the economists who attacked the book engaged with its underlying methodology. They did not build counter-models. They did not run alternative simulations. They did not challenge the structural logic of feedback, accumulation, and delay. They objected to the conclusions, not the architecture. As the systems analyst Ugo Bardi later observed, many of the book's most prominent critics had never examined the model at all.

There was a deeper reason for the hostility. The entire edifice of post-war economics was built on the assumption that growth could and should continue indefinitely. Growth was not merely a desirable outcome; it was the organising principle of modern governance. Fiscal policy, monetary policy, pension systems, sovereign debt structures, corporate valuations — all depended on the presumption of perpetual expansion. A model that said growth was structurally unsustainable was not just intellectually inconvenient. It was existentially threatening to the institutions and careers that depended on the opposite assumption.

Forrester, characteristically, was unsurprised by the reaction. He had encountered the same pattern with *Urban Dynamics*. Audiences would become increasingly hostile as they worked through the model's implications, because the implications challenged policies in which they were personally and politically invested. The lesson of policy resistance applied to the reception of the model itself: the system — in this case, the community of professional economists and policymakers — resisted information that contradicted its own structural assumptions.

As John Sterman would later put it, the public did not lack information about limits. It lacked the mental models necessary to interpret that information correctly.

Overshoot: The Dynamics of Delay

Whatever one thinks of the specific projections in *The Limits to Growth*, the structural insight at its core has never been refuted. That insight can be stated in a single paragraph.

In any system where a stock is growing exponentially and the constraints on that growth are subject to delay, the stock will overshoot the sustainable level before the constraint takes effect. The longer the delay, the greater the overshoot. And the greater the overshoot, the sharper the eventual correction.

This is not a political claim. It is a mathematical consequence of the interaction between exponential growth and delayed feedback. It applies to populations of bacteria in a petri dish. It applies to leveraged financial positions in a margin account. It applies to the concentration of greenhouse gases in the atmosphere. And it applies, as we shall see, to the accumulation of sovereign debt in a monetary system that has removed the constraints that once limited its growth.

The mechanism is always the same. A reinforcing loop drives growth. A balancing loop should, in principle, slow that growth as a constraint is approached. But the balancing loop operates with a delay. During the delay, the reinforcing loop continues to drive the stock upward. By the time the balancing signal arrives, the stock has already exceeded the sustainable level. The correction, when it comes, is not gentle. It is abrupt, because the accumulated momentum of the reinforcing loop must now be reversed.

Donella Meadows captured this dynamic with a homely analogy. On an icy road, she wrote, your car might slide past a stop sign. At a party, you might drink more alcohol than your body can safely metabolise; in the morning you will have a ferocious headache. Construction companies periodically build more condominiums than are demanded, forcing them to sell below cost. Too many fishing boats are constructed, and fleets grow so large that they catch far more than the sustainable harvest. In each case, the system overshoots because the signal that should constrain behaviour arrives too late.

The implications for monetary systems are direct, though the *Limits* team never drew them explicitly. If the supply of money or credit is a stock, and that stock grows in response to a reinforcing loop — say, the political incentive to stimulate economic activity — while the balancing loop that should constrain that growth — say, the discipline imposed by convertibility to a scarce physical asset — is weakened or removed, then the conditions for overshoot are structurally present. The stock will grow. The consequences will be delayed. And the correction, when it arrives, will be correspondingly severe.

We are not yet at the point in this book where we examine that specific case. But the reader should register the structural template. Overshoot is not a prediction. It is a dynamic that arises whenever exponential growth meets delayed constraint. The only question is which constraint, in which system, with what delay.

What the Model Missed

The most important limitation of *The Limits to Growth* was not that it was too pessimistic. In many respects, the evidence of the subsequent fifty years suggests it was too optimistic: the "standard run" scenario — the business-as-usual projection — has tracked observed data with uncomfortable accuracy. A 2008 study by the physicist Graham Turner at CSIRO in Australia compared thirty years of empirical data against the model's twelve scenarios and found that the real world was following the standard run closely. A 2020 update confirmed the same pattern. A 2023 recalibration using data through 2022 showed the overshoot-and-collapse mode still operative.

The most important limitation was, rather, one of framing. The model was built around physical variables: tonnes of resources, hectares of arable land, parts per million of pollutant. These are real and important. But they are not the only variables that govern the behaviour of a complex civilisation. And they may not be the most critical.

Consider the problem from an engineer's perspective. In any control system, the quality of the system's behaviour depends not only on the physical plant — the machinery, the stocks, the flows — but on the *measuring instruments* that the system uses to monitor its own state. A thermostat that reads the wrong temperature will drive a heating system to overshoot or undershoot. A fuel gauge that drifts will cause a pilot to misjudge range. An altimeter with a systematic bias will produce controlled flight into terrain.

The measuring instrument of a modern economy is money.

Money is the signal through which billions of decentralised actors coordinate their behaviour. It is the medium in which prices are expressed, debts are denominated, savings are accumulated, and investments are evaluated. When money is stable — when a unit of currency represents a roughly constant claim on real goods and services over time — it transmits reliable information. Actors can distinguish genuine scarcity from monetary distortion. They can plan. They can save. They can invest with reasonable confidence that the future purchasing power of their returns will resemble the present.

When money is unstable — when the measuring instrument itself changes character — the signals it transmits become unreliable. Prices no longer reflect real scarcity; they reflect a blend of scarcity and monetary expansion. Debt burdens change not because productive activity has changed, but because the unit in which those debts are measured has shifted. Savings are eroded not by consumption but by dilution. The feedback loops that should constrain excess — the rising cost of borrowing, the declining return on malinvestment, the market's price discovery of genuine value — are muffled, delayed, or overridden.

The *Limits to Growth* model did not centre money as a primary variable. It tracked physical stocks and flows. It did not model the possibility that the measuring instrument itself might become elastic — that the system's own feedback signals might be systematically distorted by changes in monetary architecture.

Whether this omission was decisive is a question for historians of modelling. What matters for our purposes is the conceptual pivot it reveals. System Dynamics teaches that the behaviour of a system is determined by its structure. But the structure of a system includes not just its physical components and their feedback relationships, but the instrumentation through which the system's operators perceive their own condition. Distort the instrument and you distort the perception. Distort the perception and you distort the response. Distort the response and you amplify the overshoot.

The Binding Constraint

Every dynamic system is governed by at least one binding constraint. This is a proposition so fundamental to engineering that it is almost never stated explicitly; it is simply assumed. A bridge is constrained by the tensile strength of its materials. An engine is constrained by the energy density of its fuel. An ecosystem is constrained by the availability of its limiting nutrient. Remove the constraint, or misidentify it, and analysis drifts into irrelevance.

The great debate provoked by *The Limits to Growth* was, at bottom, a debate about the identity of the binding constraint. The book's authors argued that the constraint was physical: the finite supply of non-renewable resources and the finite capacity of the biosphere to absorb pollution. Their critics argued that the constraint was informational: that price signals and technological innovation would shift physical limits faster than the model anticipated. The optimists pointed to the Green Revolution in agriculture, the discovery of new mineral deposits, the efficiency gains of the microchip. The pessimists pointed to the accumulation of carbon dioxide, the depletion of aquifers, the collapse of fisheries.

Both sides were partly right and both were partly blind, because neither was asking the question that an engineer trained in control systems would ask first: *is the measuring instrument working?*

In a complex civilisation, the binding constraint is not necessarily the one that is most physically obvious. It may be the one that is most structurally hidden. If the monetary system — the instrument through which all economic signals are mediated — is itself subject to a reinforcing growth loop without effective balancing feedback, then the monetary architecture may be the binding constraint, even if physical resources remain abundant in the short term.

This is because distortion of the measuring instrument distorts everything measured by it. If money expands faster than the real goods and services it is supposed to represent, then every price, every debt, every valuation, every investment decision is contaminated by the expansion. The system appears to be growing when in fact part of the apparent growth is an artefact of measurement. The system appears stable when in fact it is accumulating imbalances that are masked by the very instrument that should reveal them.

A control engineer confronted with this situation would not waste time debating whether resources were running out. The engineer would walk to the instrument panel and check whether the gauges were reading true.

From the Planet to the Instrument

The trajectory of System Dynamics, from Forrester's pencil sketch on a notebook in 1956 to the global modelling project of the early 1970s, followed a consistent logic of expansion. First, factories. Then, cities. Then, the entire world. At each stage, the same principles applied: stocks, flows, feedback, delay. At each stage, the models revealed behaviour that surprised and discomfited the people operating the systems being modelled.

But there was a domain that this expansion never quite reached. Forrester modelled industrial dynamics, urban dynamics, and world dynamics. He developed a national economic model that generated a forty-to-sixty-year economic long wave — a cycle of boom and deep slump that explained the Great Depression and predicted recurring episodes of severe contraction. Yet neither Forrester nor the *Limits* team placed the structure of the monetary system itself at the centre of their analysis.

This was not an oversight born of ignorance. It was, in part, a reflection of the era. When Forrester sketched WORLD1 on that flight from Bern, the international monetary system was still nominally anchored to gold through the Bretton Woods arrangement. The dollar was convertible. The measuring instrument appeared stable. The physical constraints — resources, pollution, population — seemed more pressing than the monetary architecture through which they were mediated.

Within a year of the publication of *World Dynamics*, that architecture changed. On 15 August 1971, President Richard Nixon suspended the convertibility of the US dollar into gold. The last structural constraint on the expansion of the global money supply was removed. The measuring instrument became elastic.

The significance of this event for the System Dynamics framework is profound, though it has been surprisingly little discussed within the System Dynamics community itself. If the principles of the discipline are correct — if structure determines behaviour, if delayed feedback amplifies overshoot, if reinforcing loops without effective balancing feedback produce instability — then the removal of the gold constraint on monetary expansion is not merely a policy decision. It is a structural change to the feedback architecture of the global economy. It is, in the language of System Dynamics, the weakening of a critical balancing loop.

What happens to a system when a balancing loop is weakened? The answer is contained in everything we have discussed so far. The reinforcing loop accelerates. The stock — in this case, the stock of money and credit — accumulates. The consequences are delayed, because the system is large and the delay is long. And the overshoot, when it becomes visible, appears sudden, though it has been building for decades.

This is not yet the argument of this book. We have not yet examined the evidence. We have not yet traced the specific feedback loops, the specific accumulations, the specific delays. That work belongs to the next chapter. What we have done is establish the conceptual framework within which that evidence will be interpreted.

The framework is System Dynamics. The question is structural. And the instrument under examination is not a factory, not a city, not the biosphere, but the thing that measures all of them: money itself.

The Engineer's Question

We began the previous chapter with a distinction. Michael Saylor does not approach the world as a financier. He approaches it as an engineer.

The distinction matters because it determines which question is asked first. A financier, confronting the global economy in 2020, asks: what is the price of this asset, and where is it going? An economist asks: what is the growth rate, and how can it be sustained? A politician asks: what policy will deliver the outcome my constituents expect?

An engineer asks: what is the structure of this system, and is the measuring instrument functioning correctly?

The *Limits to Growth* project demonstrated that systems thinking could be applied at civilisational scale. Its lasting contribution was not its specific projections — though many of those projections have proved remarkably accurate — but its demonstration that the dynamics of overshoot are structural, not circumstantial. Overshoot does not require stupidity or malice. It requires only exponential growth, delayed feedback, and a binding constraint that arrives too late to prevent accumulation beyond the sustainable level.

The project's lasting omission was its failure to examine the one variable that mediates all the others: the monetary architecture of the system under study. That omission was understandable in 1970, when the measuring instrument still appeared stable. It became less understandable after 1971. And by 2020, when the world's major central banks expanded the money supply by trillions of dollars in a matter of months, it had become the defining question of the age.

We turn now to that question. What happens, structurally, to a monetary system when the constraint that limited its expansion is removed? What are the feedback loops? What are the accumulations? What are the delays? And what does the engineer's lens reveal that the financier's lens does not?

* * *

In the next chapter, we examine the structural architecture of the post-1971 monetary system through the lens of System Dynamics — and trace the feedback loops that would eventually lead a conservative public company CEO to conclude that his cash reserves were a melting ice cube.

Chapter 3

The Fiat Feedback Trap

*"By a continuing process of inflation, governments
can confiscate, secretly and unobserved, an important
part of the wealth of their citizens."*

— John Maynard Keynes

On the evening of 15 August 1971, Richard Nixon pre-empted the most popular television programme in America to deliver an eighteen-minute address from the Oval Office. The broadcast interrupted Bonanza, a Western about a ranching family navigating life on the Nevada frontier. The irony was almost too neat. What Nixon announced that night was itself a kind of frontier event: the moment when the post-war monetary order, painstakingly assembled at Bretton Woods in 1944, was dismantled in a single presidential decree.

Nixon told the nation he was "temporarily" suspending the convertibility of the United States dollar into gold. The measure was never reversed. What happened on that August evening was the removal of a negative feedback loop, the mechanism that had, however imperfectly, constrained the expansion of the money supply since the end of the Second World War. The consequences of that removal would take decades to unfold. But by the time they became fully visible, the architecture of global money had been transformed beyond recognition, and the measuring instrument that the entire world economy depended upon had become something its designers at Bretton Woods would not have recognised.

The previous chapter ended with a question: what happens, structurally, to a monetary system when the constraint that limited its expansion is removed? This chapter provides the answer. It traces the feedback loops, the accumulations, and the delays that have governed the behaviour of the post-1971 monetary order. The diagnosis that emerges is not a moral argument about reckless central bankers or corrupt politicians. It is an engineering observation about what happens when a control system loses its governor.

The Architecture of Bretton Woods

The monetary system that Nixon dismantled had its origins in a conference held at the Mount Washington Hotel in Bretton Woods, New Hampshire, in July 1944. Seven hundred and thirty delegates from forty-four allied nations gathered in the White Mountains to design the post-war international monetary order. The war in Europe had not yet ended. The delegates could hear, through the tall windows of the hotel's Gold Room, the distant sound of the Ammonoosuc River running over granite. The central question before them was deceptively simple: how should currencies relate to one another, and what should anchor their value?

The intellectual contest at the heart of the conference pitted John Maynard Keynes, representing Britain, against Harry Dexter White, representing the United States. Keynes proposed an international clearing union with a synthetic reserve currency he called the "bancor," designed to impose symmetric adjustment obligations on both surplus and deficit nations. White proposed a system anchored to the dollar. American economic supremacy settled the matter. In 1944, the United States held roughly two-thirds of the world's monetary gold. What emerged from Bretton Woods was built on American gold and American power.

The system that the delegates constructed was a hierarchy of constraint. Other nations would peg their currencies to the dollar at fixed exchange rates, adjustable only with the consent of the newly created International Monetary Fund. The dollar, in turn, was pegged to gold at a fixed rate of thirty-five dollars per ounce. Foreign central banks (though not private citizens) could present dollars to the United States Treasury and demand gold in return. The system thus created a chain of accountability: individual nations could not debase their currencies without devaluing against the dollar, and the United States could not debase the dollar without watching its gold reserves walk out the door.

The gold window functioned, in System Dynamics terms, as a negative feedback loop. When the United States expanded its money supply beyond what its gold reserves could credibly support, foreign central banks exercised their convertibility right. Gold flowed out of Fort Knox. This created a stock-depletion signal: as the gold reserve diminished, it provided an unmistakable, physically measurable warning that monetary expansion had exceeded its structural limit. The signal was visible. It was quantifiable. And unlike an inflation statistic, which could be redefined, seasonally adjusted, or simply argued about, it was impossible to ignore. A vault that is emptying speaks with a clarity that no committee communiqué can match.

The system was not perfect. It placed enormous strain on the United States, which bore the simultaneous burden of maintaining domestic economic policy and international monetary discipline. The economist Robert Triffin identified the central paradox as early as 1960: the world needed a growing supply of dollars to facilitate expanding international trade, but producing those dollars required the United States to run persistent balance-of-payments deficits, which gradually undermined confidence in the dollar's gold backing. The very success of the system contained the mechanism of its eventual failure.

A System Dynamics practitioner would recognise the structure immediately. Triffin had identified a reinforcing feedback loop embedded within what appeared to be a stable architecture. The more the system succeeded in promoting global trade, the more dollars it required. The more dollars the United States produced, the weaker the gold anchor became. The weaker the anchor, the more fragile the confidence that sustained the entire arrangement. The loop was self-amplifying, and its endpoint was predictable to anyone who understood the direction of the flow.

The Night the Governor Was Removed

By the late 1960s, the strain had become acute. The cost of the Vietnam War and President Johnson's Great Society programmes had driven a substantial expansion of federal spending, financed in large part by monetary creation. Foreign central banks, led by France under Charles de Gaulle, began exercising their convertibility rights with increasing vigour. De Gaulle made no secret of his contempt for what his finance minister, Valéry Giscard d'Estaing, had famously called America's "exorbitant privilege," the ability to settle international debts in a currency only the United States could print. In 1965, in a gesture calibrated for maximum symbolic effect, France dispatched a naval vessel to New York to collect its gold. The message was unmistakable.

Between 1959 and 1971, United States gold reserves fell from approximately 20,000 tonnes to fewer than 9,000. The stock was draining. The feedback signal was clear. But the political cost of responding to that signal (by cutting domestic spending or raising interest rates in the midst of a war abroad and ambitious social programmes at home) was deemed unacceptable. Nixon faced a choice that systems engineers understand well: obey the governor, or remove it.

He removed it.

The "temporary" suspension of gold convertibility was announced alongside wage and price controls and an import surcharge, bundled together as the "New Economic Policy." The political framing was masterful. Nixon presented the measures as a defence of the American worker against "international money speculators." The stock market rallied the following day by the largest single-day percentage gain in decades. Editorial opinion was broadly favourable. Treasury Secretary John Connally, a Texan whose confidence was commensurate with his state, told a gathering of European finance ministers: "The dollar is our currency, but it's your problem." The immediate crisis was resolved.

What was lost, however, was the constraint mechanism itself. From August 1971 onwards, the dollar, and by extension every currency pegged to it, was backed by nothing other than the policy discretion of its issuing government. The stock of gold in Fort Knox was no longer relevant to monetary operations. The flow of dollars into the global economy was no longer subject to an external physical limit. For the first time in modern history, every major currency on earth was a pure fiat instrument, its value determined entirely by the judgement and discipline of the institutions that controlled its supply.

The monetary system had been converted from a closed-loop control system, in which output was constrained by measurable physical feedback, to an open-loop system, in which output was constrained only by the intentions of the operator. Any engineer will tell you what happens next. Open-loop systems are inherently vulnerable to drift, because they possess no self-correcting mechanism independent of the operator's judgement. If the operator misjudges the environment, or faces incentives that conflict with system stability, there is nothing in the structure itself to prevent deviation from accumulating. The system does not know it has drifted. It has no instrument to tell it so. That instrument was gold, and it has been disconnected.

The Elastic Reserve

The consequences of this structural change did not manifest immediately. Indeed, for the first decade, they manifested in a form that appeared to confirm the critics' worst fears and then, paradoxically, to refute them. Inflation surged through the

1970s, driven by the combination of loose monetary policy, two oil price shocks, and the collapse of the anchoring expectations that Bretton Woods had provided. By 1980, consumer price inflation in the United States had reached nearly fifteen per cent per annum. Mortgage rates exceeded eighteen per cent. The post-war economic order appeared to be unravelling.

Then Paul Volcker intervened. Appointed chairman of the Federal Reserve in August 1979, Volcker raised the federal funds rate to twenty per cent, an act of monetary violence without precedent in the post-war era. The resulting recession was deep and painful. Unemployment rose above ten per cent. Farmers drove tractors onto the National Mall in protest. Congressmen introduced legislation to impeach Volcker. But the inflationary spiral broke. By the mid-1980s, inflation had fallen below four per cent, and it would remain low for a generation.

The apparent success of the Volcker intervention reinforced a seductive narrative: that competent central bankers, armed with the right models and sufficient institutional independence, could manage a fiat currency as effectively as gold had once anchored it. Discretion, the argument ran, was superior to constraint. A wise pilot was better than an autopilot. The gold standard, in this telling, was a relic of a less sophisticated age, a crude mechanical governor rendered obsolete by the advancement of macroeconomic science.

The data tells a more complicated story. In 1971, the total United States money supply, measured by the broad M2 aggregate, stood at approximately $685 billion. By 2000, it had grown to $4.9 trillion. By 2020, on the eve of the pandemic, it had reached $15.4 trillion. By April 2020, following the Federal Reserve's emergency response to COVID-19, it had surged past $18 trillion. As of early 2024, it stands above $21 trillion. These figures are denominated in the very unit that is being expanded, which gives them an air of unreality, like measuring the growth of a river using a ruler that is itself dissolving in the current.

Stated differently: the money supply expanded by a factor of roughly thirty in just over fifty years. No physical quantity in the real economy, whether population, productivity, industrial output, or resource extraction, grew by a comparable multiple over the same period. United States real GDP roughly quadrupled. The population roughly doubled. The money supply multiplied by thirty. The gap between the growth of the monetary stock and the growth of the real economy it was supposed to measure is the central structural fact of the post-1971 monetary order. The pattern is neither conspiracy nor aberration, but the predictable behaviour of a stock whose inflow has been structurally liberated from the constraint that once governed it.

The stock-and-flow pattern is straightforward. The stock of money is increased by inflows: new money creation through bank lending, central bank asset purchases, and fiscal deficits monetised by the banking system. It is decreased by outflows: loan repayments, defaults, and the occasional deliberate contraction of the central bank's balance sheet. Since 1971, the inflows have consistently and dramatically exceeded the outflows. The stock has grown relentlessly, punctuated by brief and partial reversals that have never come close to restoring the prior level.

None of this represents a failure of the system. The system is working as designed. The gold anchor was removed precisely so that monetary authorities could expand the supply of money when they judged it necessary. The problem is not that the operators were incompetent, though some were. The problem is that the incentive structure of the system itself favours expansion over contraction, always and everywhere, for reasons that are structural rather than personal.

The Ratchet: Why Contraction Fails

To understand why fiat monetary systems exhibit persistent inflationary bias, one must examine the asymmetry of the political feedback loops that govern them. This asymmetry operates at every level of the system and creates what amounts to a structural ratchet: easy to turn in one direction, almost impossible to turn in the other.

Consider the position of a central banker confronted with an economic slowdown. The immediate pressure (from financial markets, politicians, the press, the public) is to ease monetary conditions: to lower interest rates, to expand lending, to inject liquidity. The benefits of easing are immediate and visible. Markets rally. Borrowing costs fall. Businesses invest. Hiring resumes. The central banker is praised for decisive action. The consequences of easing (the gradual erosion of purchasing power, the inflation of asset prices relative to wages, the accumulation of debt that will constrain future flexibility) are diffuse, delayed, and difficult to attribute to any single decision. They emerge over years and decades, distributed across millions of transactions, and by the time they become visible, the policymaker who authorised the original expansion is long out of office.

Now consider the reverse. When the economy overheats and inflation rises, the central banker must tighten: raise rates, restrict lending, withdraw liquidity. The costs of tightening are immediate and visible. Markets fall. Borrowing costs spike. Businesses contract. Workers lose jobs. Home buyers are priced out of the mortgage market. The central banker is blamed, personally and publicly, for causing a recession. The benefits of tightening (the restoration of price stability, the correction of speculative excess, the rebuilding of room for future manoeuvre) are diffuse, delayed, and accrue to a future that the current electorate does not yet inhabit.

The asymmetry is brutal in its implications. The political rewards of expansion arrive quickly and are credited to the policymaker. The political costs of contraction arrive equally quickly and are also credited to the policymaker. But the costs of expansion and the benefits of contraction are separated from their causes by years or decades of delay. This is a textbook case of what System Dynamics calls policy resistance, operating through what Sterman's research programme has identified as the fundamental attribution error of dynamic systems: the tendency to react to proximate symptoms while ignoring the structural causes that produced them.

The central banker may genuinely intend to maintain price stability. But the feedback loops surrounding each decision (short-term political pressure rewarding expansion, long-term consequences of expansion arriving too late to discipline the original choice) create an environment in which the rational response, at every individual decision point, is to err on the side of more money rather than less. Each crisis triggers an expansion. Each expansion is only partially reversed before the next crisis arrives. The base level of money in the system rises with each cycle. The ratchet turns. And it turns in one direction.

The Great Moderation and the Illusion of Mastery

The period from the mid-1980s to the mid-2000s came to be known, with characteristic hubris, as the Great Moderation. Macroeconomic volatility appeared to have been conquered. Recessions were mild and brief. Inflation was low and stable. Growth was steady. Central bankers were lionised. In 2004, Ben Bernanke, then a governor of the Federal Reserve and not yet its chairman, delivered a lecture celebrating the achievement and attributing it to improved monetary policy, structural changes in the economy, and, with a modesty that would soon appear tragically misplaced, a degree of good fortune. The chairman of the Federal Reserve, Alan Greenspan, was treated in Washington and on Wall Street with a deference usually reserved for heads of state. He was called "The Maestro." A journalist wrote a book with that title. Greenspan did not object.

The intellectual foundation of this confidence was the belief that central banks had learned to manage the fiat system, that the absence of a gold anchor did not matter, because institutional competence and sophisticated modelling had replaced the need for a mechanical constraint. The economy, in this view, was a complex but ultimately manageable machine that could be tuned by adjusting a few key parameters: the federal funds rate, the reserve requirement, the scale of open market operations. The science of monetary policy, its practitioners believed, had matured.

What the Great Moderation masked was the accumulation of structural fragility beneath the surface of apparent stability. During those calm decades, several trends were compounding quietly. Total United States household debt rose from roughly $1.5 trillion in 1980 to over $12 trillion by 2007. Financial innovation was creating increasingly complex instruments (mortgage-backed securities, collateralised debt obligations, credit default swaps) that distributed risk in ways that were poorly understood even by the institutions that traded them. The Federal Reserve, under Greenspan and later under Bernanke, had developed a pattern of intervening aggressively to cushion every significant market downturn: the Mexican peso crisis of 1994, the collapse of Long-Term Capital Management in 1998, the bursting of the dot-com bubble in 2000. The pattern became known as the "Greenspan put": an implicit guarantee that the central bank would always step in to prevent asset prices from falling too far. The guarantee was never formally stated. It did not need to be. Markets are adept at reading structural incentives.

The Great Moderation was, in System Dynamics terms, a classic case of delayed feedback concealing a reinforcing loop. The apparent stability was not evidence that the system had been tamed. It was evidence that the consequences of the system's structural imbalances had not yet arrived. The debt stock was growing. The complexity of financial instruments was increasing. The implicit guarantee of central bank intervention was encouraging ever-larger risk exposures. The feedback signal that should have warned of mounting danger, the price of money itself expressed through interest rates and credit spreads, was being actively suppressed by the very institution charged with maintaining stability.

The parallel with the previous chapter is striking. This fits the overshoot dynamic described in the previous chapter. The Meadows team modelled systems in which a stock accumulates behind a delayed feedback signal, overshooting its sustainable level before the signal arrives. The Great Moderation was exactly such a system. The stock of debt and leveraged risk accumulated for two decades. The feedback signal, the market's own price discovery of risk, was suppressed by the Greenspan put. The sustainable level was exceeded long before the correction came. And when it came, the correction was not gentle.

2008: The Signal Arrives

When the reckoning came, it arrived with a violence that surprised almost everyone except those who had been watching the stocks rather than the flows. The collapse of Lehman Brothers on 15 September 2008 triggered a cascade of failures across the global financial system. The intricate web of counterparty obligations, which had been presented as a sophisticated mechanism for diversifying risk, proved instead to be a transmission network for systemic contagion. Banks that had appeared solvent on Friday were insolvent by Monday. The global interbank lending market, the plumbing through which the world's financial institutions settle their daily obligations, seized up entirely. For several days in late September and early October, the machinery of global finance came closer to complete cessation than at any point since the 1930s.

The Federal Reserve's response was unprecedented in scale. Interest rates were cut to near zero. Emergency lending facilities were established for institutions that had never before received direct central bank support. And then came quantitative easing: the direct purchase of financial assets by the central bank, funded by the creation of new reserve balances, money conjured into existence by an entry on a digital ledger. Between 2008 and 2014, the Federal Reserve's balance sheet expanded from approximately $900 billion to $4.5 trillion. The Bank of England, the European Central Bank, and the Bank of Japan undertook comparable programmes. The scale of the intervention was, in historical terms, without parallel.

The immediate crisis was resolved. The financial system was stabilised. Catastrophe was averted. But the mechanism of stabilisation was, in structural terms, an intensification of the very dynamic that had produced the crisis. The system had become unstable because of excessive debt accumulation, the mispricing of risk, and the suppression of corrective feedback signals. The response was more debt creation, further suppression of risk signals, and interest rates held at the zero lower bound for seven years. Asset prices recovered and then exceeded their pre-crisis levels. The stock of money in the system expanded dramatically. The ratchet turned again.

There was a grim irony in this. The lesson of 2008, stated plainly, was that the financial system had accumulated risks that its operators did not understand, in quantities that its structure could not absorb. The policy response was to ensure that the operators retained their positions, the structure remained intact, and the accumulation resumed. The fire was extinguished by soaking the building in the same fuel that had ignited it.

2020: The Acceleration

The pattern repeated, at an accelerated tempo, in March 2020. The arrival of the COVID-19 pandemic triggered a sharp economic contraction as governments around the world imposed lockdowns of varying severity. The Federal Reserve's response made its 2008 intervention look tentative by comparison. In a matter of weeks, the central bank cut rates to zero, launched unlimited quantitative easing (the word "unlimited" was used explicitly, a first) and established lending facilities for corporate bonds, municipal securities, and exchange-traded funds, backstopped money market funds, and reopened emergency swap lines with foreign central banks. The federal government, enabled by the Federal Reserve's asset purchases, ran fiscal deficits of peacetime magnitudes not seen since the founding of the republic.

The scale was extraordinary. The Federal Reserve's balance sheet, which had taken six years to expand from $900 billion to $4.5 trillion during and after the 2008 crisis, expanded from $4.2 trillion to nearly $9 trillion in approximately two years. The M2 money supply, which had grown by roughly $3 trillion in the decade following 2008, grew by over $6 trillion in two years. Approximately forty per cent of all dollars in existence at the end of 2021 had been created since the beginning of 2020. This statistic, widely cited at the time, was not precisely accurate in every formulation, but its directional force was undeniable: the monetary stock had undergone a step-change expansion of a kind normally associated with wartime mobilisation or the fiscal emergencies of developing economies.

Once again, the immediate crisis was managed. The economy recovered. Markets surged to new highs. But the structural consequences, this time, could not be concealed by delay. Inflation, which had been dormant for so long that a generation of economists had begun to theorise that it might never return, reappeared with a force that caught policymakers visibly off guard. Consumer prices in the United States rose at rates not seen since the early 1980s. The Federal Reserve, which had spent much of 2021 characterising the inflation as "transitory," was forced into a belated and aggressive tightening cycle, raising interest rates at the fastest pace in four decades.

The tightening itself produced casualties. In March 2023, Silicon Valley Bank, the sixteenth-largest bank in the United States, collapsed in a matter of hours after rising interest rates destroyed the market value of its bond portfolio, triggering a depositor run that social media accelerated to a speed no previous bank run had achieved. Signature Bank and First Republic followed within weeks. Each failure required emergency intervention: a new facility, a new guarantee, a new public assurance that the system was sound. The Federal Deposit Insurance Corporation quietly extended what amounted to unlimited deposit protection, a guarantee that had not been authorised by Congress and whose cost had not been disclosed to the public. The ratchet turned once more.

The Structural Diagnosis

Viewed through the lens of System Dynamics, the post-1971 monetary system exhibits a clear and consistent behavioural pattern. It is a system with a dominant reinforcing loop and a progressively weakened, in some respects deliberately disabled, balancing loop.

The reinforcing loop operates as follows. Monetary expansion produces short-term economic growth and rising asset prices. Rising asset prices increase collateral values, which support further lending. Further lending increases the money supply. The expanded money supply flows disproportionately into financial assets, driving prices higher still. The cycle repeats. Each iteration leaves the system with a larger stock of money and a larger stock of debt. The two grow in tandem, because in a fiat system, most money is created through the extension of credit: one person's deposit is another person's loan.

The balancing loop that should constrain this process, the mechanism by which excessive expansion is detected and corrected, has been progressively weakened at each stage of the story. The gold window was the original, physical constraint; it was removed in 1971. Market discipline, the prospect that reckless expansion would be punished by falling bond prices, rising yields, and the withdrawal of investor confidence, was undermined by the Greenspan put and its successors. Inflation targeting, which was supposed to provide a rule-based anchor in the absence of gold, proved too flexible in practice: targets were redefined, measurement methodologies were adjusted, timelines were extended, and the word "transitory" was invoked whenever the data proved inconvenient.

The result is a system that trends, structurally and relentlessly, towards monetary expansion. Not because the people operating it are malicious or incompetent, but because the architecture rewards expansion and punishes restraint. The feedback that should govern the system arrives too late, lands on the wrong people, and is systematically overridden by political incentives that operate on shorter time horizons than the consequences they produce.

The claim is not ideological but observational: it concerns the behaviour of a system with known structural properties. A system with asymmetric incentives, delayed negative feedback, and no hard external constraint on the growth of its primary stock will drift in the direction of least resistance. In the case of money, that direction is always more.

The Measurement Problem

There is one further consequence of this structural drift that demands attention, because it bears directly on the argument of the chapters that follow. When the unit of measurement itself is expanding, it becomes progressively more difficult to measure anything else accurately.

Prices in a fiat system do not merely reflect supply and demand for goods and services. They also reflect changes in the supply of money. When the money supply expands, prices rise, but not uniformly and not simultaneously. Asset prices tend to respond first and most dramatically, because financial markets are closest to the point of money creation. Real estate follows, mediated by the credit channel. Consumer prices respond last, because they are constrained by wage contracts, supply chain frictions, competitive pressures, and the simple fact that most people cannot raise the prices they charge as easily as a central bank can expand the money it creates. The result is that the same monetary expansion produces wildly different effects in different parts of the economy, and at different times, and is therefore extraordinarily difficult to perceive as a single, unified phenomenon.

For the individual saver, this creates a quiet catastrophe. The purchasing power of money held in a bank account declines steadily, year after year, at a rate that is difficult to perceive in the short term but devastating over decades. A dollar saved in 1971 retains less than fifteen cents of its original purchasing power today. The loss is not dramatic enough to provoke political action in any given year. But compounded over a working lifetime, it represents an enormous, silent transfer of wealth from those who hold money to those who borrow it and those who own the assets whose prices rise with the monetary tide. This is not a distributional side-effect of the system. It is the system's most consistent output.

For the corporate treasurer, the problem is more immediate and more measurable. A company holding significant cash reserves watches those reserves lose real value with each passing quarter. The larger the reserve, the greater the loss. No hedge exists within the fiat system for this risk, because the system itself is the source of the debasement. Every instrument denominated in fiat currency shares the same fundamental exposure: its value is contingent on the discipline of institutions whose structural incentives favour expansion over restraint, whose track record of restraint is, over any multi-decade period, unbroken in its absence.

The System and Its Behaviour

The post-1971 monetary system is not broken in the sense that it has malfunctioned. It is operating precisely as its structure dictates. The feedback loops that govern it produce exactly the outcomes that a System Dynamics analysis would predict: persistent expansion of the monetary stock, periodic crises when the accumulated imbalances can no longer be concealed, emergency interventions that resolve immediate instability at the cost of amplifying the underlying dynamic, and a ratcheting baseline that rises with each cycle.

The governor was removed in 1971. No equivalent has been installed since. The system has been running without one for over half a century. And the consequences of that absence are now so deeply embedded in the structure of global finance, so thoroughly woven into the expectations of every participant, that restoration of an external constraint would itself constitute a systemic shock of the first order. The ratchet, in other words, does not merely resist reversal. It has made reversal almost unthinkable.

This is the structural environment into which Bitcoin was born. And it is the structural environment that one particular engineer, watching from a corporate office in northern Virginia in the spring of 2020, examined through the lens of stocks, flows, feedback, and delay, and concluded that his company's cash reserves were not a store of value at all, but a melting block of ice, losing mass with every passing quarter, and that the only rational response was to find something that would not melt.

That engineer, and his decision, are the subject of the next chapter.

* * *

Chapter 4

The Melting Reserve

"Energy is the only universal currency. One of its many forms must be transformed to get anything done."

— Vaclav Smil

Michael Saylor was born in 1965 on a military base in Lincoln, Nebraska. His father was a chief master sergeant in the United States Air Force, and the family moved frequently during Saylor's childhood, following postings across the country and to bases in Japan and New Zealand. The itinerant life of an Air Force family instils certain habits: adaptability, self-reliance, and a respect for institutional discipline that coexists, in the more independent-minded children, with an instinct for working the system rather than being passively shaped by it. Saylor displayed the latter tendency early. He was the valedictorian of his high school class and won an Air Force ROTC scholarship to MIT, where he would study aeronautics and astronautics alongside the history of science, technology, and society.

It was at MIT, as described in Chapter 1, that Saylor encountered System Dynamics. The encounter shaped everything that followed. But the immediate path after graduation did not lead to a career in systems modelling. It led, briefly, to the Air Force. Saylor was commissioned as a Second Lieutenant upon graduation in 1987. His intention was to fly jets. A benign heart murmur, discovered during his flight physical, closed that path. The cockpit he had trained for was denied to him. He pivoted to consulting, building computer simulations for industrial clients (DuPont, Dow, Exxon), and then, at the age of twenty-four, to entrepreneurship.

He founded MicroStrategy in 1989, in Tysons Corner, Virginia, with a single employee and a contract from DuPont. He had been out of MIT for two years.

The company he built was a business intelligence firm, a maker of software that helped large organisations interrogate their own data, find patterns in operational noise, and make decisions on the basis of what the numbers actually said rather than what managers believed them to say. It was, in other words, a company whose founding purpose was the correction of flawed mental models through structured analysis. The intellectual inheritance from Forrester and Sterman was not abstract. It was the product.

The early years were lean. Saylor ran the company from a basement office in the Virginia suburbs of Washington, in Tysons Corner, a sprawl of office parks and shopping centres that no one would mistake for Silicon Valley. He coded, sold, hired, and evangelised with an intensity that those who worked with him in that period recall as both galvanising and exhausting. Semu Mulugeta, MicroStrategy's co-founder, provided the technical counterweight: quieter, more methodical, less inclined to grand pronouncements. The partnership worked. MicroStrategy grew steadily through the early and mid-1990s on the back of contracts with government agencies and Fortune 500 companies who needed to make sense of the data they were generating in ever-larger quantities.

By the late 1990s, the company had gone public. Saylor, who retained a large equity stake, had become a billionaire on paper. He was thirty-four years old. The business press noticed. Saylor, with his MIT pedigree, his rapid-fire conversational style, and his willingness to make sweeping claims about the transformative power of technology, became a fixture on the conference circuit. He gave a speech in which he predicted that the internet would destroy every university in America. He was photographed at parties. He bought a yacht. In the overheated atmosphere of the dot-com boom, where every technology CEO was treated as a visionary and every business model was assumed to work until it didn't, Saylor fit the era perfectly.

The Dot-Com Wreck

What happened next would have destroyed a less stubborn man. In March 2000, at the peak of the bubble, MicroStrategy disclosed that it had materially overstated its revenues for two fiscal years. The company had been recognising revenue from long-term software contracts prematurely, booking future income as though it had already been earned. The restatement was severe. Revenues for 1999, originally reported at $205 million, were revised downward to $150 million. The stock, which had traded above $300 per share in early March and had briefly touched $333, collapsed. Within days it had fallen below $100. By midsummer it was below $40. By the end of the year it was in single digits.

The speed of the destruction was staggering. Saylor's personal fortune, which had peaked at approximately $13.5 billion in early March 2000, making him briefly one of the twenty wealthiest people on earth, was effectively wiped out within a month. The Guinness Book of World Records would later cite his loss as the largest personal financial loss in a single day in history. Whether or not the record is precisely accurate, the directional force of the statistic is undeniable.

The Securities and Exchange Commission opened a formal investigation. Saylor, along with the company's chief financial officer and its former chief operating officer, was charged with financial fraud. The SEC alleged that MicroStrategy had systematically overstated revenues and understated losses in order to meet analyst expectations and maintain the stock price. The case was settled in December 2000 without an admission or denial of guilt. Saylor paid a $350,000 fine and accepted a cease-and-desist order. He was not barred from serving as an officer or director of a public company. He stayed.

The decision to stay was the most revealing act of Saylor's career up to that point. Most Silicon Valley narratives, when they touch on disgrace at all, pivot to a redemption arc involving a new venture and a fresh start: the chastened founder moves to a different city, launches a different company, and earns a second fortune that obliterates the memory of the first. Saylor did none of this. He remained at MicroStrategy. He remained in Tysons Corner. He rebuilt the company from within, slowly, quarter by quarter, from the rubble of the restatement.

The accounting failure was real and serious. But the underlying business, the software itself, was sound. MicroStrategy's platform did what it was supposed to do: it helped large organisations analyse large data sets. The customers who used it valued it. The stock had been destroyed by a loss of market confidence, not by a loss of product capability. Saylor set about restoring the first while continuing to develop the second.

The rebuild was slow, unglamorous, and largely ignored by a technology press that had moved on to the next cycle of enthusiasm. Through the early 2000s, MicroStrategy shed staff, renegotiated contracts, and focused on generating cash from its existing customer base. The company that had once embodied the swagger of the late-nineties tech boom became something closer to a utility: reliable, profitable in a modest way, and invisible. Saylor, once the subject of fawning profiles in business magazines, disappeared from public view almost entirely. He ran his company. He paid down obligations. He accumulated cash.

The Conservative Balance Sheet

The experience of the dot-com crash and the SEC investigation shaped Saylor's approach to corporate finance in ways that would prove decisive two decades later. Having watched his company nearly die from a combination of aggressive accounting, market mania, and the sudden withdrawal of investor confidence, he adopted a posture of extreme financial conservatism. MicroStrategy would carry no significant debt. It would generate free cash flow from operations. It would accumulate liquid reserves. The balance sheet would be a fortress, and the fortress would never again depend on the goodwill of equity markets for its survival.

This philosophy was tested, severely, in 2008. The financial crisis that followed the collapse of Lehman Brothers was the worst economic contraction since the Great Depression. Credit markets froze. Banks that had reported healthy capital ratios weeks earlier discovered that their assets were worth a fraction of their book value. Companies across every sector scrambled for liquidity, cutting staff, selling assets, drawing down credit lines. Those without reserves discovered, in the space of a few terrifying weeks in September and October, what it meant to depend on the willingness of counterparties to extend credit during a panic. The willingness was not forthcoming.

MicroStrategy, sitting on its growing cash pile, watched the carnage from a position of safety. The company continued to operate, continued to pay its employees, continued to serve its clients. It did not need to borrow. It did not need to sell assets at distressed prices. It did not need to go to the capital markets with a begging bowl. Saylor's two decades of financial conservatism, dismissed by some analysts as overcautious and capital-inefficient, had proved their worth in the only way that mattered: the company survived without distress while others did not.

The lesson reinforced itself with each quarterly cash flow statement. In a world prone to periodic convulsions whose timing cannot be predicted, the prudent corporate strategy was to stockpile liquidity and avoid leverage. Every dollar of free cash flow that was not needed for operations or product development went into the reserve. The fortress grew.

By early 2020, three decades of this philosophy had produced a company with an unusual financial profile. MicroStrategy was profitable but modestly so. Its software business generated reliable but unspectacular revenue, roughly $500 million per year, serving a loyal base of enterprise clients in sectors (government, retail, financial services) where analytical software was embedded in daily operations and switching costs were high. The company's market capitalisation was approximately $1.2 billion. And it held, in cash and short-term investments, approximately $500 million.

Half a billion dollars in liquid reserves for a company of that size was, by any normal corporate standard, an excess. The cash exceeded what was needed for operations, for capital expenditure, for product development, for any plausible acquisition. It was, in effect, a corporate savings account. Saylor had spent twenty years building it, dollar by dollar, quarter by quarter, out of operating cash flow and the discipline of a man who had once watched everything evaporate. It was the product of patience and a deeply held conviction that reserves were safety.

Then, in March 2020, he began to question whether what he had built was safe at all.

The Thermodynamic Insight

The COVID-19 pandemic arrived in the United States in late February and early March 2020. Within weeks, governments imposed lockdowns of varying severity across every major economy. Economic activity contracted at a speed without modern precedent. The policy response, as described in the previous chapter, was a monetary and fiscal expansion of historic proportions. The Federal Reserve cut rates to zero, launched open-ended asset purchases, and established lending facilities across the full spectrum of credit markets. The federal government passed relief packages measured in trillions. The combined effect was the largest peacetime expansion of the monetary base in the history of the dollar.

Saylor watched this unfold from his office in Tysons Corner. He was not watching the stock market. He was watching the money supply.

The distinction matters. A financier watches prices. An engineer watches rates of change. Saylor had been trained at MIT to think in stocks and flows, to track accumulations rather than spot values, and to ask not where a variable stands today but what structural forces will determine where it stands in five, ten, or twenty years. The variable he was tracking in March 2020 was M2, the broadest commonly reported measure of the dollar money supply, and its rate of expansion had shifted from a walk to a sprint.

In a series of conversations that summer with colleagues, board members, and a widening circle of people who were thinking about the same problem, Saylor began to articulate what he was seeing in thermodynamic language. Energy, he argued, is the fundamental unit of economic value. Human labour is energy. Capital goods embody stored energy. Money is supposed to capture and preserve economic energy over time, in the same way that a battery stores electrical charge. A sound monetary instrument preserves the energy deposited in it. An unsound one leaks.

The analogy was not casual. Saylor returned to it repeatedly in public appearances over the following months, refining the language with each iteration. In thermodynamics, an adiabatic system is one in which no energy is lost to the surrounding environment. A perfectly adiabatic container preserves everything placed inside it indefinitely. Saylor's contention was that a sound money, a money with a fixed and unalterable supply, would function as an adiabatic store of economic energy: what you put in is what you get out, regardless of how much time passes. Fiat currency, by contrast, was a leaky container. The rate of leakage was the rate of monetary expansion, and in 2020 that rate had lurched upward.

The "melting ice cube" metaphor, which Saylor used in his first major public interview about the decision, captured the same idea in less technical form. An ice cube left on a kitchen counter does not shatter or explode. It simply loses mass, slowly and continuously, until it ceases to exist. The process is undramatic. At any given moment the change is barely perceptible. But the direction is irreversible and the endpoint is zero. Cash held in a fiat currency, Saylor argued, behaved in the same way. Its nominal value remained unchanged on the balance sheet. Its real purchasing power diminished with every expansion of the money supply. And the rate of expansion, as the events of 2020 demonstrated, could accelerate sharply and without warning.

Saylor ran the numbers on MicroStrategy's own position. Half a billion dollars in cash, eroding at whatever rate the Federal Reserve's expansion implied for long-run purchasing power dilution. Even on conservative assumptions (five to seven per cent annual real erosion), the loss was substantial: $25 to $35 million per year, invisible on the income statement, absent from any regulatory disclosure, but compounding relentlessly. Over a decade, on less conservative assumptions, the cumulative loss could approach half the original sum. The reserves accumulated over twenty years of disciplined management could lose half their real value without a single adverse event occurring, without a lawsuit filed or a customer lost, simply as the unit of account in which the reserves were denominated expanded around them.

For a man who had spent his career building software to help companies see through the noise in their own data, the realisation had a bitter clarity. The most important number on his own balance sheet was lying to him. The cash line showed $500 million. The real value of that cash, measured in future purchasing power, was something less. And it was declining.

The Search for a Constrained Asset

Having diagnosed the problem, Saylor surveyed the available alternatives with the methodical intensity of an engineer evaluating competing designs. The search was driven by a specific set of criteria derived from the structural analysis. He needed an asset that could absorb a large allocation of corporate capital without moving the market against him; that would preserve or increase its purchasing power over long time horizons; that could be held on a public company balance sheet without introducing unmanageable operational or regulatory complexity; and whose supply was subject to a credible, externally verifiable, non-discretionary constraint.

Real estate was considered and rejected. Property is illiquid, jurisdiction-dependent, subject to variable taxation and regulation, and requires ongoing management expertise. For a technology company with no property operations, a large real estate allocation would introduce risks and competencies unrelated to the core business.

Gold was considered more seriously. It met some of the criteria: scarce, historically durable, broadly recognised as a store of value across civilisations and centuries. But it failed others. Physical gold requires custody, insurance, and verification. Gold-backed financial instruments reintroduce the counterparty risk that the allocation is meant to escape. And gold's supply, while constrained by geology, is not fixed. New mining production adds roughly 1.5 to 2 per cent to the above-ground stock each year. Over multi-decade horizons, this dilution compounds. Gold is scarce but not immutable.

Equities were considered and rejected on different grounds. A large equity portfolio held as a treasury reserve converts a software company into, in part, an investment fund. It introduces exposures to sectors, management teams, and economic cycles unrelated to MicroStrategy's business. It creates governance complications: a company holding a diversified equity portfolio must explain to shareholders why management is better positioned to pick stocks than the shareholders themselves. And equities, while they can generate real returns, remain denominated in the fiat currency whose debasement is the problem being addressed. They hedge the symptom, not the cause.

Bitcoin, when Saylor turned his attention to it in the summer of 2020, was not an asset he had previously taken seriously. In a 2013 tweet, widely circulated after the MicroStrategy announcement, he had dismissed it bluntly, predicting that its days were numbered. The reversal was total, and Saylor made no attempt to conceal or minimise it. He had been wrong, he said. He had not understood the protocol. He had confused Bitcoin's price volatility with structural weakness, and had not examined the supply mechanism with the rigour it deserved.

His re-education, by his own account, occupied several hundred hours of reading, conversation, and analysis during the spring and summer of 2020. He read Saifedean Ammous's *The Bitcoin Standard*. He studied the protocol's technical documentation. He spoke with developers, with long-term holders, with institutional investors who had already made smaller allocations. He applied the same analytical method he had used in his MIT thesis: identify the structural features of the system, model their behaviour over time, and assess whether the architecture produces the outcomes it claims to produce.

What he found appeared to satisfy the criteria that the alternatives could not. Bitcoin's supply was capped at twenty-one million units by the protocol itself, a constraint enforced not by policy or promise but by the consensus rules of a distributed network running open-source code. Its issuance schedule was predetermined, transparent, and had operated without deviation since the network launched in January 2009. It was liquid: traded twenty-four hours a day, seven days a week, on markets spanning every major jurisdiction. It could be held on a corporate balance sheet as a digital asset without requiring warehouses, insurance policies, or custodial infrastructure of the kind that physical commodities demand.

The volatility was obvious and could not be dismissed. Bitcoin's price had fallen by more than fifty per cent on multiple occasions in its twelve-year history. For a corporate treasurer accustomed to the soporific stability of a money market fund, this was alarming. But Saylor's analysis drew a distinction between volatility and structural risk that most observers were not making. Volatility is the fluctuation of price around a trend. Structural risk is the degradation of the trend itself. Cash offered low volatility but carried structural risk: its purchasing power was in long-term decline and the decline was accelerating. Bitcoin offered high volatility but, if the protocol held, zero structural dilution. The supply could not be expanded by committee decision, emergency decree, or political convenience.

The choice, as Saylor framed it in his conversations with the board that summer, was between a slowly melting asset that never fluctuated and a volatile asset that could not melt. The conventional treasury held certainty of gradual loss. The unconventional treasury held uncertainty of direction but certainty of supply.

The Board Decision

Saylor did not act alone. MicroStrategy was a public company with a board of directors, institutional shareholders, legal counsel, auditors, and fiduciary obligations. Converting half a billion dollars of treasury reserves into an asset that most of the financial establishment regarded as speculative required more than conviction. It required persuasion, due diligence, and the willingness of independent directors to attach their reputations to a decision that had no corporate precedent.

The process, as Saylor described it in subsequent interviews, began with education. He assembled the analysis he had been developing since March: the monetary expansion data, the purchasing power calculations, the structural comparison between fiat and fixed-supply assets, the survey of alternatives and the reasons each had been rejected. He presented the case to his board not as a wager on Bitcoin's price appreciation but as a reassessment of the risk profile of their existing treasury. The framing was critical. Saylor was not asking the board to speculate. He was asking them to recognise that what they had considered their safest asset was, on a long enough timeline, their most exposed one.

The board deliberated. Legal and accounting implications were examined in detail. The question of fiduciary duty was central: could directors justify allocating corporate treasury to an asset as volatile as Bitcoin? Saylor's answer inverted the conventional risk assessment. Fiduciary duty, he argued, required directors to preserve shareholder value. Holding an asset demonstrably losing real value, while the rate of loss accelerated, could itself constitute a failure of that duty. The reckless act, in this framing, was not to buy Bitcoin. It was to sit on a pile of melting cash and do nothing.

On 11 August 2020, MicroStrategy announced that it had purchased 21,454 bitcoins for approximately $250 million, at an average price of roughly $11,653 per coin. The press release described Bitcoin as "a dependable store of value and an attractive investment asset with more long-term appreciation potential than holding cash." The language was measured, almost bland. It gave no indication of the analytical intensity that had preceded it, nor of the scale of what would follow.

A second purchase followed in September: 16,796 additional bitcoins for approximately $175 million. By December 2020, MicroStrategy had committed nearly all of its cash reserves to Bitcoin. The company that had spent twenty years accumulating a fortress balance sheet had, in the space of four months, converted that fortress into something the financial world had never seen before: a public corporation whose primary treasury asset was a twelve-year-old cryptographic protocol.

The Public Reaction

The initial market response was muted. MicroStrategy was a mid-cap enterprise software company with a modest public profile, trading at a market capitalisation that barely registered against the technology giants that dominated the headlines. Its first Bitcoin purchase attracted attention in cryptocurrency circles but was noted only briefly by the mainstream financial press. The second purchase drew more notice. By the time Saylor began giving extended interviews in late 2020, explaining the reasoning in the thermodynamic and systems-thinking language that came naturally to him, the reaction had shifted from indifference to polarisation.

Critics were abundant and vocal. The allocation was called reckless, irresponsible, a violation of prudent corporate governance. Analysts questioned whether MicroStrategy's board had fulfilled its fiduciary obligations. Short sellers took positions against the stock, arguing that the company had transformed itself from a software business into a leveraged Bitcoin bet. The Wall Street consensus, to the extent one existed, was that Saylor had taken leave of his senses, that the SEC crisis of 2000 should have taught him humility, and that the volatility of the underlying asset would eventually vindicate the doubters.

Supporters were fewer but emphatic. Within the Bitcoin community, Saylor's decision was treated as vindication of a thesis that had been circulating for years: that Bitcoin's fixed supply made it a superior store of value, and that institutional adoption was only a matter of time. Saylor was an MIT graduate with a systems-analysis background who had independently arrived at the same conclusion. His conversion (the word was used deliberately, with its overtones of religious awakening) gave institutional credibility to an argument that had previously been confined to cryptography forums and libertarian podcasts.

Saylor embraced the public role with a vigour that surprised even those who knew him. He gave hundreds of interviews. He hosted a conference, "Bitcoin for Corporations," aimed at corporate treasurers and CFOs considering similar allocations, and attracted thousands of attendees. But the most sustained and revealing exposition of his thinking came in a series of extended conversations with the podcaster Robert Breedlove, recorded in late 2020 for Breedlove's programme *The What is Money Show*.

The conversations, which became known as the Saylor Series, ran to seventeen episodes and approximately twenty-five hours of recorded dialogue. Saylor later recalled that he had expected the conversation to last a couple of hours. "I never really thought much about what is money until you asked me," he told Breedlove at the book launch. "And then we sat down for this podcast, I thought it'd be a couple of hours, and it turned out to be eighteen hours or something like that." The outline for the entire series, he said, was extemporaneous: he reeled off a set of topics in the first hour and the rest unfolded from there, unprepared and unscripted.

The scope of what emerged was remarkable. Saylor began not with Bitcoin, not with money, not even with economics, but with the Stone Age. His argument ran as follows. Human civilisation advances by mastering successive forms of energy. Fire was the first great breakthrough: the harnessing of chemical energy, the ability to cook food, to clear land, to survive cold. Missiles were the second: the channelling of kinetic energy, from the thrown rock to the spear to the bow to the Balearic slinger who could put a lead bullet through a man's skull at five hundred metres. Hydraulics were the third: the redirection of gravitational energy through dams, canals, and irrigation. Each leap forward was a leap in the capacity to channel energy across space and time.

From these Palaeolithic foundations, Saylor built outward through the Dark Ages, the invention of the printing press, the economic logic of the Reformation ("Martin Luther," he observed, "had an economic impetus as well as a theological one; it's useful to have God on your side"), the rise and fall of empires centred on great cities (Venice, Amsterdam, Manhattan), the steel revolution that made modern civil engineering possible, the food networks of the industrial age, and the conquest of infectious disease by antibiotics. He paused at Hershey, Pennsylvania, to explain how Milton Hershey's chocolate factory was essentially a clean-room facility for stabilising food energy at room temperature, and he paused at the Great Wall of China to quote Philip II of Macedon: "No citadel is impenetrable as long as it has a road wide enough for me to fit a donkey up it with a pot of gold on its back." The meaning, Saylor noted, was that no defence, however physically formidable, can withstand monetary corruption from within.

The intellectual breadth was not decorative. Each historical digression served a structural purpose: to establish that the story of civilisation is the story of energy capture, storage, and transmission, and that money is the highest-order form of that energy. "Money is the highest form of energy that human beings can channel," Saylor stated in the fourth episode. "When I first started thinking about money as an energy system, it led me to ask the question: what were the formative energy systems of the human race?" The question drove the entire arc of the series, from Palaeolithic fire to Bitcoin's proof-of-work algorithm.

The climax of the argument was thermodynamic. Saylor contended that a sound monetary system must respect the laws of physics, specifically the conservation of energy: "Bitcoin is a cyber economy based upon the principles of truth, respecting the laws of thermodynamics, respecting Newton's laws. If you're going to worship the goddess of energy, you'd better respect the laws of conservation of energy." On another occasion, speaking to Lex Fridman, he brought the point home with a nautical analogy: if a ship leaks two per cent of its volume per year, its useful life is fifty years. A wooden ship, in other words. Build the same vessel from steel and the degradation rate falls to zero. The analogy was direct: a fiat currency that inflates at two per cent per year has a useful half-life of thirty-five years. A fixed-supply protocol has none. The engineering comparison was not casual. It was the entire point.

In July 2022, the Saylor Series was published as a book, *What Is Money? The Saylor Series*, a 403-page transcript of the conversations edited by Seth Simmons. It was available in paperback, hardback, and Kindle editions. The format was unusual: a transcribed dialogue, essentially a Socratic exchange in which Breedlove asked questions and Saylor answered at length, with summary points appended to each chapter. It was not polished prose. It had the looseness and the repetitions of extemporaneous speech. But the intellectual force of the argument, built from first principles over twenty-five hours, gave it a cumulative weight that more conventional treatments of Bitcoin lacked. Breedlove summarised the central theme at the book launch: "How human beings channel energy across space and time toward the achievement of their goals." Saylor, characteristically, wanted the audience to take something practical from it: "I hope people get some value from this and find ways that they can use it to inspire people around them or improve their own lives."

The significance of the Saylor Series for the broader Bitcoin proposition was substantial. Before Saylor, the intellectual case for Bitcoin had been made primarily in technical, economic, or libertarian terms. Saifedean Ammous's *The Bitcoin Standard* had framed the argument through Austrian economics. The cypherpunk tradition had framed it through cryptography and privacy. Saylor framed it through the history of science and technology, through thermodynamics and the philosophy of engineering, and in doing so gave the proposition an intellectual heft that reached audiences who would never have picked up a book on Austrian monetary theory. A CEO who could move in a single paragraph from Balearic slingers to Newton's laws to the conservation of energy to the Federal Reserve's balance sheet was not easy to dismiss as a speculator or a crank. The argument could be challenged on its merits. But it could not be waved away.

If the Breedlove dialogues provided depth, it was the podcast ecosystem at large that provided reach. One of the first serious long-form interviews Saylor gave after the August announcement was with Peter McCormack on *What Bitcoin Did*, then already one of the most widely listened-to Bitcoin podcasts in the world. McCormack was a British former digital marketing entrepreneur who had discovered Bitcoin in 2017 and built the podcast, over the following three years, into a weekly programme with over a million monthly listeners. His interviewing style was direct, unpretentious, and unafraid of asking the question that a technically sophisticated audience might consider naive. For Saylor, whose natural mode was the extended analytical monologue, McCormack provided something valuable: a conversational counterweight that forced the argument into plain language.

The two would record at least four major interviews between 2020 and 2024. In the first, recorded in October 2020 and titled "Bitcoin in the Boardroom," Saylor walked through the mechanics of the treasury conversion in detail: the Dutch auction he offered to shareholders uncomfortable with the strategy, the board deliberations, the accounting treatment. In a later episode, recorded in Miami in November 2021 with MicroStrategy's Bitcoin holdings then worth several billion dollars, Saylor declared himself "five hundred per cent exposed," a formulation that captured the escalating scale of the commitment. McCormack later described Saylor as "the walking encyclopedia." In a 2023 episode, Saylor spent part of the conversation giving careers advice to McCormack's son, a detail that speaks to the informal warmth that developed between the two men despite their very different backgrounds.

McCormack's own trajectory is worth a brief digression, because it illustrates something about the distributed, non-institutional character of the network through which Saylor's thesis reached its widest audience. McCormack had no economics training, no finance background, no university degree in a relevant discipline. He had struggled with cocaine addiction. He had rebuilt his life around a podcast and, in 2021, around a football club: he purchased Bedford FC, a non-league side in Bedfordshire, rebranded it as Real Bedford, dressed the players in bright orange kits bearing the Bitcoin logo, and declared his intention to take the club to the Premier League, funded in part by a Bitcoin treasury. The Winklevoss twins invested $4.5 million and became co-owners in 2024. When McCormack announced the club's Bitcoin acquisition on Twitter, Saylor replied with two words: "Real ₿edford." The exchange was brief, but it captured the peculiar ecosystem that had formed around the MicroStrategy thesis: a world in which a billionaire software CEO in Virginia and a podcaster running a tenth-tier football club in the English Midlands were participants in the same monetary argument, connected by a protocol and a shared conviction about its significance.

Saylor, who had spent two decades in the relative obscurity of enterprise software, had become the most prominent corporate advocate for Bitcoin in the world. He had also, perhaps less willingly, become a lightning rod. Every swing in Bitcoin's price was now refracted through the lens of MicroStrategy's balance sheet. A rally was vindication. A crash was recklessness. The man who had retreated into anonymity after the dot-com disaster had, for the second time in his life, made himself inseparable from the fate of a volatile asset. The question was whether the structural analysis that had driven the decision would prove more durable than the market's mood.

Whether this public role was calculated or compulsive, strategic or temperamental, is a question that those who write his biography will eventually have to settle. What can be said with confidence is that the intellectual framework was consistent. From the Machiavelli thesis of 1987 to the Bitcoin allocation of 2020, the analytical method had not changed: identify the structural features of a system, model their long-run consequences, and act on the model rather than on the consensus. The method had nearly destroyed him in 2000. In 2020, he bet the company on it again.

The Melting Ice Cube, Revisited

The phrase "melting ice cube" entered the financial lexicon after Saylor used it in his early interviews about the MicroStrategy decision. It was effective because it captured, in a domestic image, a dynamic that is otherwise difficult to perceive. Inflation, in its modern form, does not announce itself with wheelbarrows of devalued currency or queues outside banks. It operates through the quiet, cumulative erosion of purchasing power, visible only in retrospect: in the house that costs ten times what it cost a generation ago, in the pension that buys less each year, in the savings account that grows in nominal terms and shrinks in real ones.

Saylor's contribution was to reframe this familiar observation as an engineering problem with an engineering solution. The ice cube metaphor is not a complaint about central bankers or a prediction of monetary collapse. It is a description of a rate of change. If the rate of monetary expansion exceeds the rate of real economic growth, the difference represents a transfer of value from holders of money to issuers of money and to those who receive newly created money first. The transfer is continuous, compounding, and over long periods, large. For an individual saver, the transfer is painful but survivable. Wages adjust, imperfectly and with delay, but they adjust. For a corporation sitting on hundreds of millions of dollars in cash, the arithmetic is less forgiving. Corporate cash does not earn wages. It sits. And as it sits, it melts.

The decision to convert MicroStrategy's treasury was, at its core, a refusal to accept that melting as inevitable. The fiat monetary system, as described in the previous chapter, is structurally predisposed to expansion. The expansion dilutes existing holders. The dilution is a feature of the architecture, not a malfunction. But the fact that a system is working as designed does not oblige every participant to remain within it. An engineer who identifies a structural deficiency in a system is not obligated to continue operating inside that system without modification. The engineer can look for an exit.

Whether Bitcoin constitutes a viable exit is a question the remaining chapters will examine. What can be established here is the logic of the search and the coherence of the decision that followed from it. Saylor did not wake up one morning and decide to buy Bitcoin on a whim. He diagnosed a structural problem in the instrument his company used to store value. He surveyed alternatives against specific criteria. He identified an asset whose supply characteristics addressed the deficiency he had diagnosed. And he committed to it with a decisiveness that reflected either deep conviction or deep recklessness, depending on where one stands.

* * *

In the next chapter, we follow the strategy from diagnosis to execution. How does a public company CEO, having concluded that his treasury is a melting asset, construct a corporate machine to acquire a fixed-supply alternative at scale, financed not from operating cash flow but from the capital markets themselves?

Chapter 5

The Network and the Attractor

*"Throughout history, hierarchies housed in high
towers have claimed to rule, but often real power has
resided in the networks in the town square below."*
— Niall Ferguson, The Square and the Tower

The first four chapters of this book have established a specific kind of argument. Chapter One introduced the analytical lens: System Dynamics, the engineering habit of mind, structure determining behaviour. Chapter Two demonstrated that lens operating at civilisational scale — the *Limits to Growth* project, the overshoot dynamic, and crucially, the omission that would prove most consequential: the monetary instrument itself was never modelled. Chapter Three filled that omission, tracing the post-1971 monetary architecture as a system with a dominant reinforcing loop and a progressively disabled balancing constraint. Chapter Four brought the argument to a single human actor: Saylor, the MIT engineer who looked at his corporate balance sheet through a systems lens and concluded that cash was a melting asset.

There is a risk, at this juncture, that the book becomes a corporate biography of an unusually thoughtful man. It is a risk worth naming directly, because the remedy requires a deliberate shift of register. Saylor's diagnosis was correct. His analysis was rigorous. His courage, in converting half a billion dollars of corporate reserves into an asset that the financial establishment regarded as speculative, was considerable. But he was not the first person to see the destination. He arrived at Bitcoin through the engineering lens of thermodynamics and monetary debasement — brilliantly, and very publicly. A decade before he converted his treasury, however, another figure had looked at the same emergent system from an entirely different vantage point and reached a structurally compatible conclusion by a different route.

That figure is Marc Andreessen.

The Man Who Built the Browser

To appreciate the weight of Andreessen's argument, it is necessary to understand who he is and what he has already seen. He is not a monetary theorist. He is not an economist. He is, in the most direct sense, someone who watched a new technology protocol emerge from obscurity, propagate through adoption waves, generate network effects that compounded upon themselves, and ultimately become indispensable infrastructure for a civilisation that had not requested it, could not have predicted it, and today cannot function without it.

He watched this happen because he helped make it happen. In 1993, as a twenty-two-year-old undergraduate at the University of Illinois, Andreessen co-wrote Mosaic, the first widely used web browser. He then co-founded Netscape, the company that brought the World Wide Web to a mass audience. He was present, in the most literal sense, at the creation. He saw what the early internet looked like when it was still fringe: technically functioning, intellectually compelling to a small community of enthusiasts, and almost universally dismissed by the establishment as a toy for academics and cryptographers. He saw the adoption curve inflect. He watched a protocol that the mainstream had ignored become the substrate of global commerce. And he retained, with unusual clarity, the memory of what dismissal looked like in the years before that inflection.

When Andreessen published his essay "Why Bitcoin Matters" in the *New York Times* in January 2014, he was not performing the role of cryptocurrency evangelist. He was performing the role of a man who had experienced, at close quarters, the early stages of a previous technological revolution and recognised in Bitcoin a structural pattern he had seen before. His opening framing was precise: a mysterious new technology emerges, apparently out of nowhere, but actually the result of years of intense research and development by relatively unknown researchers. Political idealists project utopian visions onto it. Establishment players — banks, regulators, media commentators — ridicule the proposition. Technical sceptics identify every flaw. And all the while, the network keeps growing.

The language is familiar, because the language describes what happened to the internet. But Andreessen was not making a metaphorical point about cultural reception. He was making a structural one. The comparison to the early internet was not rhetorical comfort for Bitcoin believers. It was a hypothesis about adoption dynamics: that open protocols with permissionless participation, strong network effects, and genuine utility follow a characteristic trajectory regardless of the establishment's opinion of them. The establishment's opinion, he observed, is usually the same at every stage. It is usually wrong.

Network Effects and the Logic of Compounding

To understand why Andreessen's argument is more than analogy, it is necessary to examine the mechanism he was invoking, because that mechanism has a precise structural character that connects directly to the systems analysis of the preceding chapters.

A network effect is what happens when a product or service becomes more valuable to each of its users as more people use it. The telephone is the canonical example. A single telephone is worthless. Two telephones constitute a communication channel. A million telephones constitute an infrastructure. The value does not increase linearly with the number of users. It increases, as the mathematician Robert Metcalfe observed, approximately in proportion to the square of the number of connected users. Each new participant does not add their own individual value to the network. They add a connection to every other participant already present. The network grows, and its utility grows faster.

A systems analyst would recognise this immediately. A network effect is a reinforcing feedback loop. The stock of participants increases the utility of the network. The utility of the network drives the inflow of new participants. The inflow increases the stock. The loop is self-amplifying, and its output compounds. This is not merely a convenient metaphor borrowed from engineering. It is the literal structure of what is happening when a network expands under the influence of its own adoption dynamics.

The consequences of this structure are non-linear and, in their early stages, invisible. Below a critical threshold, a network's value proposition is marginal and its adoption is slow. The reinforcing loop is operating, but its output is too small to attract attention. The network appears to be going nowhere. Then the stock of participants crosses a threshold, the loop begins to operate at a scale where its compounding is visible, and adoption accelerates. The inflection point, when it arrives, appears sudden. It is not. It is the cumulative product of the loop's quiet operation across many prior periods, in the same way that the overshoot crises described in Chapter Three appeared sudden to observers who had not been watching the stocks accumulate.

Andreessen understood this because he had watched it happen with the internet, and he saw in Bitcoin the same structural signature. An open protocol. Permissionless participation. A network whose utility to each participant increased with the size of the total participating network. And, critically, a governance architecture that no single actor could capture or corrupt — a property that, as we shall see, has a specific and important bearing on the question of where the network's adoption curve ultimately arrives.

The Square and the Tower

At roughly the same time that Andreessen was articulating his network-effects case for Bitcoin, the historian Niall Ferguson was developing an argument about the structure of historical power that would, when eventually published as *The Square and the Tower* in 2017, provide one of the most illuminating frameworks for understanding what Bitcoin represents in civilisational terms.

Ferguson's central argument is architectural. Throughout history, he contends, power has resided in one of two kinds of structure: the tower or the square. The tower represents hierarchy — vertical, concentrated, organised around chains of command and control, capable of the efficient exercise of power in stable conditions but brittle in the face of rapid change, and fundamentally dependent on maintaining information asymmetry to sustain its authority. The square represents the network — horizontal, distributed, organised around voluntary association and mutual benefit, capable of generating innovation and spreading ideas with a speed that hierarchies cannot match, but historically vulnerable to eventual co-option or suppression by the hierarchies that perceive it as a threat.

The history Ferguson tells is one of oscillation between these two modes. The printing press broke the Catholic Church's control of information and created the distributed network of the Reformation. A century of violent conflict followed. Then the hierarchies regrouped: first the Peace of Westphalia, then the centralisations of the nineteenth century, in which new technologies — the telegraph, the railway, the steamship — served not to distribute power but to concentrate it further in the hands of states and their institutions. The Soviet Union represented the apogee of hierarchical power: a system that tolerated no parallel networks, that attempted total vertical control, and that ultimately collapsed not because it ran out of natural resources but because it could no longer suppress the horizontal connections that any sufficiently complex society generates.

The internet inaugurated what Ferguson calls the Second Age of Networks. Information asymmetry — the tower's most reliable weapon — became structurally difficult to maintain. Ideas that hierarchies would once have suppressed could now propagate through horizontal channels faster than any institutional response. The Arab Spring offered one demonstration of this dynamic. Social media offered another. And then something more fundamental appeared: not merely a network for sharing information, but a network for transmitting value, operating entirely outside the tower's jurisdiction.

Ferguson's framework illuminates Bitcoin in a way that neither Saylor's thermodynamic language nor conventional economic analysis quite captures. The existing monetary system is a tower structure in the most precise sense. It is hierarchical, vertical, and organised around a single point of control: the central bank. Its authority depends on the absence of alternatives. For as long as there is no credible means of storing and transmitting value outside the banking system, the tower's monopoly on the money supply is absolute. Remove the gold constraint, as Nixon did in 1971, and the tower's discretionary power over the monetary stock becomes effectively unlimited. The system described in Chapter Three — the ratchet, the reinforcing loop without effective balancing feedback, the structural drift toward expansion — is the predictable behaviour of a tower that has neutralised every external constraint on its own authority.

Bitcoin is a square phenomenon. It emerged not from a central bank, not from a financial institution, not from a government laboratory, but from an anonymous white paper published to a cryptography mailing list in October 2008 — the very month that the tower's most spectacular modern failure was unfolding in the collapse of Lehman Brothers. Its architecture was designed with explicit structural intent: to create a value network that required no central authority, that enforced its own rules through the distributed consensus of its participants, and that could not be captured by any single actor, however powerful, without the agreement of the network itself. It is, in Ferguson's terms, a network that the tower cannot reach.

Why Hierarchies Cannot Capture Bitcoin

Ferguson's historical analysis contains a cautionary note that deserves serious engagement. Networks, he observes, have a persistent structural vulnerability: over time, they tend to form up into hierarchies. The forces that drive this consolidation are familiar — the gains from scale, the efficiencies of centralised coordination, the political incentives that accrue to those who can position themselves as essential nodes in a widely used network. Christianity began as a distributed network of small communities sharing a radical message. Within three centuries, it had become the most durable hierarchy in the history of Western civilisation. The internet began as a distributed network of universities and research laboratories. Within two decades, its commercial layer had consolidated around a handful of platforms whose network effects made them near-impossible to dislodge.

The question this history raises for Bitcoin is pointed: why should this network be different? Why should the protocol that emerged from the cryptography underground in 2008 not follow the same trajectory as every previous network — initial distribution, growing adoption, and gradual consolidation into a new kind of tower, perhaps more sophisticated in its architecture but functionally equivalent in its concentration of control?

The answer lies in the specific design choices embedded in Bitcoin's protocol, and it is here that the system dynamics analysis of the preceding chapters connects to Ferguson's historical framework in a way that neither author made explicit. The standard failure mode of networks — the route by which they become hierarchies — is the accumulation of discretionary control over a critical shared resource. The Catholic Church accumulated doctrinal authority. The internet platforms accumulated data. Central banks accumulated the power to expand the monetary stock. Each consolidation followed from control over a bottleneck: a resource that network participants required and that could be rationed, restricted, or modified by whoever controlled it.

Bitcoin's protocol was engineered to eliminate this bottleneck. The supply is capped at twenty-one million units by a rule enforced not by any institution or governance body but by the mathematical consensus of the distributed network itself. There is no committee that can vote to expand the supply. There is no regulator that can instruct the protocol to issue more coins. There is no Volcker moment — no individual authority whose personal conviction can override the structural constraint. The governor, in the System Dynamics language of Chapter Three, is not a policy choice. It is an architectural feature. It cannot be removed by political pressure because there is no political mechanism capable of doing so. The tower cannot reach it.

This is the property that makes Bitcoin's network dynamics structurally different from those of every previous network that Ferguson describes. The consolidation path that Christianity and the internet both followed required capturing control of a discretionary resource. Bitcoin was deliberately designed to have no discretionary resource to capture. The network can be adopted by institutions — and it has been, with increasing speed since 2020. But adoption is not capture. An institution that adds Bitcoin to its treasury is participating in the network on the network's terms. It is not acquiring the ability to modify those terms. The tower can enter the square. It cannot become the square.

The Inflection and the Attractor

This brings us to the structural argument that connects Andreessen's network effects, Ferguson's historical framework, and the System Dynamics analysis that has been the analytical spine of this book.

In systems with strong reinforcing feedback loops, the long-run behaviour of the system is governed by its attractor states: configurations toward which the system naturally tends under the influence of its own internal dynamics. A ball placed anywhere on the inside of a bowl will, if released, roll toward the bottom. The bottom is the attractor state. It is not that the ball is trying to reach the bottom. It is that the structure of the bowl makes the bottom the only stable resting place. Every other position is unstable; every perturbation returns the ball toward the centre. The bowl's geometry determines the ball's destiny.

The argument of this chapter, stated plainly, is that the monetary architecture described in Chapter Three creates the conditions for exactly this kind of attractor dynamics. A monetary system whose supply constraint has been removed is a system permanently tilted away from stability. The reinforcing loop — expansion, asset inflation, further expansion — has no natural terminus. It will continue to operate until an external constraint reimposed from outside the system brings it to rest. Historically, that external constraint has taken the form of a fixed-supply asset whose scarcity could not be inflated away: gold, land, productive capital. In each case, the flight from debasement found the same kind of destination: something that could not be printed.

Bitcoin is a fixed-supply asset whose scarcity is enforced not by geology or geography but by protocol. Its supply constraint is more absolute than gold's — no new mining production above the schedule, no discretionary authority that can adjust the issuance rate. And it combines this supply constraint with the adoption dynamics that Andreessen identified: network effects that compound with each new participant, strengthening the network's utility and pulling in the next cohort of adopters.

The two dynamics operate on different axes but reinforce one another. On the supply axis, Bitcoin's architecture produces increasing scarcity as adoption grows and the fixed supply is distributed across a larger number of holders. On the demand axis, Bitcoin's network produces increasing utility as adoption grows and the network becomes more liquid, more trusted, and more widely accepted as a settlement layer. Supply constrained, demand expanding: in any asset market, this combination produces a single directional force. And in a world where the alternative — the fiat monetary system — is structurally configured to produce the opposite dynamic, the attractor state becomes clearly visible.

A systems analyst looking at this configuration would make the following observation. The post-1971 monetary system is a dynamic with a dominant reinforcing loop and no effective governor. Left to run, it will continue to expand the monetary stock, eroding the purchasing power of existing holders and driving capital toward assets that offer protection from that erosion. Bitcoin is an asset with a hard supply cap and a demand-side reinforcing loop. In a world of monetary expansion, it is structurally positioned to capture the flight from debasement that the monetary system itself generates. The system, in other words, produces its own antidote. Not by design. By structure.

Saylor's Role: Threshold, Not Origin

With this framework established, we can return to Michael Saylor and locate him with greater precision in the story being told.

Saylor was not the person who identified the attractor state. Andreessen identified it, at least in outline, in 2014, through the lens of network effects and the structural analogy with the early internet. Ferguson identified the civilisational context: the tower's structural vulnerability to a network it cannot capture. The cryptographic tradition that produced Bitcoin's protocol had identified the technical architecture required to make the supply constraint credible. What Saylor contributed was something different and, in terms of the system's adoption dynamics, more important.

He crossed a threshold.

In System Dynamics, complex systems often exhibit what Sterman calls threshold behaviour: a reinforcing loop operates below the level of institutional visibility for years, gathering momentum, and then a critical stock level is reached. At that point, the loop begins to operate at a scale where its effects become undeniable to actors who had previously been able to ignore them, and the behaviour of the system shifts. The threshold is not a cause. It is a tipping point in a dynamic that was already in motion. Before the threshold, the loop's output is too small to compel institutional response. After it, the loop's output is too large to ignore.

When MicroStrategy announced its initial Bitcoin purchase in August 2020, the network of institutional actors who had been monitoring Bitcoin with cautious interest, but deferring adoption pending evidence that the proposition was viable at institutional scale, received a signal they had been waiting for. A NASDAQ-listed company with a credible chief executive, an MIT engineering background, and a track record of rigorous analysis had concluded, after months of structured due diligence, that converting corporate treasury reserves to Bitcoin was not reckless but prudent. The Dutch auction Saylor offered to dissenting shareholders, the board deliberations, the legal and accounting frameworks developed to support the allocation — each of these constituted, for the institutional world watching from the sidelines, a demonstration that the proposition was actionable. The threshold had been crossed. The adoption loop accelerated.

What followed is a matter of record. Square, Tesla, and a succession of hedge funds made allocations within months. Institutional custody solutions proliferated. Regulated Bitcoin exchange-traded products emerged in the United States. Sovereign wealth funds began disclosing exposures. The language of the conversation shifted: Bitcoin moved from the vocabulary of speculation to the vocabulary of treasury management, asset allocation, and macroeconomic hedging. None of this would have been impossible without Saylor. The structural forces described in this chapter would have continued to operate. But his public commitment — and the analytical rigour with which he explained it — shortened the timeline by demonstrating the institutional viability of the proposition at precisely the moment when the macroeconomic conditions made it most compelling.

Andreessen saw the network before the network was large enough to see itself. Ferguson described the civilisational stakes without naming the specific asset. Saylor provided the institutional template at the moment the system crossed its threshold. Three observers, three vantage points, three contributions to a single structural argument. The argument is not about the price of Bitcoin. It is about the architecture of two competing monetary systems — one governed by discretionary authority operating through a tower of interlocking institutions, the other governed by protocol operating through a distributed network in the square below — and about which of those architectures the long-run dynamics of adoption and flight from debasement will select.

The engineer's answer is the same as the network analyst's and the historian's. Structure determines behaviour. The tower, having removed its own governor, has been expanding its monetary stock for more than half a century. The square, having designed a network whose supply constraint cannot be removed, has been compounding its adoption dynamics for fifteen years. The attractor state is not a prediction. It is what the structure of the two systems, examined honestly and without sentiment, appears to produce.

* * *

In the next chapter, we examine the execution of Saylor's strategy in detail: how a public company chief executive, having diagnosed the monetary system as a structural source of treasury erosion and identified Bitcoin as the engineered antidote, constructed a corporate machine to acquire it at scale — not from operating cash flow, but from the capital markets themselves. The strategy that followed was, in its own way, as structurally elegant as the argument that produced it.

Chapter 6

The Conservative Case

> *"The problem in this world is to avoid concentration of power. We must have a dispersion of power. If I am against government intervention, it is because I am in favour of freedom."*
>
> — Milton Friedman

The word conservative carries, in the monetary context, two entirely distinct meanings that are rarely brought into alignment. The first is political: the instinct, running from Edmund Burke through Friedrich Hayek and Milton Friedman to the governing programmes of Margaret Thatcher and Ronald Reagan, that governments cannot be trusted with unconstrained power over the money supply, that sound money is a precondition of a free society, and that the inflation of currency is not merely an economic inconvenience but a form of confiscation — a tax levied on savers without legislation, without debate, and without the public's consent. The second meaning is older and more elemental. It is thermodynamic. A conservative asset is one that conserves what is deposited in it. It does not leak. It does not degrade. It preserves value across time in the way that a well-engineered vessel preserves its contents: not through policy, not through the good intentions of its custodians, but through the properties of its own architecture.

The argument of this chapter is that these two meanings converge in Bitcoin, and that their convergence is not accidental.

It is structural. Bitcoin is conservative in both senses simultaneously: it is the technological completion of an argument that the political right has been making, imperfectly and incompletely, for half a century, and it is an asset whose supply architecture makes it, in Saylor's thermodynamic language, the closest approximation to an adiabatic store of economic energy that human ingenuity has yet produced. To understand why these two meanings converge, and why that convergence matters, it is necessary to trace the intellectual tradition that runs from Hayek's seminal insight through Friedman's monetarism through the political projects of the 1980s — and to ask, honestly, why that tradition succeeded in breaking inflation but failed to install the architectural constraint that would have prevented its return.

The Road Hayek Built

In 1944, the same year that the delegates assembled at Bretton Woods to design the post-war monetary order, Friedrich Hayek published The Road to Serfdom. His argument was not primarily monetary. It was political and philosophical: that central planning, however benevolent its intentions, necessarily concentrated power in ways that were incompatible with individual freedom, because the planner who controlled the allocation of resources controlled, in effect, the conditions of everyone's life. The book was addressed to socialists who believed they could plan their way to prosperity. But its logic applied, with equal force, to monetary planners who believed they could manage their way to sound money.

Hayek was not blind to this implication, and he returned to it explicitly more than three decades later. In 1976, in a short but incendiary pamphlet published by the Institute of Economic Affairs, he advanced a proposition so radical that even his admirers found it difficult to take seriously. The pamphlet was titled The Denationalisation of Money, and its argument was precisely what the title suggested: that governments should be stripped of their monopoly over currency issuance, that private institutions should be free to issue competing currencies, and that the market — not the state — should determine which forms of money people preferred to use.

Hayek's reasoning began with an observation that the earlier chapters of this book have now traced in considerable structural detail. Governments, he argued, had monopolised the provision of money and then consistently abused that monopoly. Central banks, nominally independent, were in practice responsive to the fiscal needs of their governments, accommodating deficits through monetary expansion and suppressing interest rates to ease the burden of sovereign debt. The result, entirely predictable from the incentive structure, was a persistent inflationary bias. "Ministers of finance," he wrote, "were told by economists that running a deficit was a meritorious act, and even that, so long as there were unemployed resources, extra government expenditure cost the people nothing." Any effective bar to the rapid increase in government expenditure, the gold standard being the most important, had been removed. And once removed, the dynamic was self-reinforcing: governments spent, central banks accommodated, and the purchasing power of savings quietly eroded.

His remedy was competition. Allow private issuers to offer their own currencies. Allow the public to choose among them. The currencies that held their value would attract holders; those that depreciated would be abandoned. Market discipline would achieve what political discipline had consistently failed to deliver. The idea was greeted, even by sympathetic economists, with scepticism. It was widely regarded as an elegant theoretical proposition that could never be implemented in practice, because the infrastructure required to verify, settle, and account for competing private currencies simply did not exist. Hayek himself acknowledged as much, noting in later years that he regretted not having had the time to develop the proposal further.

The technology did not exist in 1976. It does now. The European Central Bank, in a 2012 report on virtual currency schemes, observed that the theoretical roots of Bitcoin could be found in the Austrian school of economics, citing as the two most relevant intellectual antecedents the gold standard tradition and Hayek's 1976 treatise. This is not a retrospective appropriation. It is a recognition that Bitcoin achieved, through cryptographic protocol, precisely what Hayek had proposed but could not implement through institutional design: a currency whose supply was governed by a rule rather than a discretion, that competed on its merits in an open market, and whose integrity depended on no single issuer's promise to behave.

Friedman's Diagnosis

Where Hayek's monetary argument was primarily institutional — focused on who should issue currency and under what constraints — Milton Friedman's was empirical. Friedman's central monetary proposition, which he first articulated in a talk delivered in India in 1963 and which became one of the most cited sentences in the history of economics, was a statement about cause: "Inflation is always and everywhere a monetary phenomenon, in the sense that it is and can be produced only by a more rapid increase in the quantity of money than in output."

The statement was not merely definitional. It was an empirical claim that cut against the dominant Keynesian consensus, which held that inflation was a cost-push phenomenon — driven by wage demands, supply shocks, and the structural features of labour markets — that could be managed through a combination of fiscal intervention and incomes policy. Friedman's counter was blunt: wherever you find sustained inflation, look first at the money supply. The diagnosis was resisted for a decade and then, in the crucible of the 1970s stagflation — when the Keynesian prescription of fiscal stimulus combined with wage controls failed to arrest the inflationary spiral — it was vindicated. Friedman received the Nobel Prize in Economics in 1976, the same year Hayek's monetary pamphlet appeared.

But Friedman's diagnosis was more structurally interesting than his remedy. His prescription — the k-percent rule, a commitment by central banks to expand the money supply at a fixed annual rate commensurate with real economic growth — was an attempt to replace discretion with rules. If the money supply grew at a stable, predictable rate, the inflationary bias embedded in the political incentive structure would be neutered. Central bankers could not expand the monetary stock beyond the rule without violating a public commitment. The rule, in System Dynamics terms, was a proposed balancing loop: a constraint that would prevent the reinforcing loop of monetary expansion from running unimpeded.

The k-percent rule was never implemented. Central banks that experimented with money-supply targeting in the early 1980s — including the Bank of England under Thatcher and the Federal Reserve under Volcker — found that the relationship between monetary aggregates and inflation was less stable than Friedman's framework assumed. The velocity of money proved unpredictable. The definition of the money supply was contested. And the political commitment required to hold the rule through recessions and crises proved, in every case, insufficient. By the mid-1980s, formal monetarist targeting had been quietly abandoned in favour of the discretionary inflation targeting that Friedman had specifically argued against. The rule was replaced by the judgement of the operator. The governor was, once again, a policy choice rather than an architectural feature.

This failure is significant for the argument of this book, but not in the way that critics of monetarism suppose. The failure was not a refutation of Friedman's diagnosis. It was a confirmation of it. The money supply expanded, as it always does when the constraint is a policy commitment rather than a structural impossibility. The purchasing power of savings eroded, as it always does when the instrument that measures economic value is itself subject to discretionary expansion. What the failure of monetarism demonstrated was not that Friedman was wrong about the cause of inflation, but that the remedy he proposed — a rule maintained by institutional commitment — was insufficient. Rules can be rewritten. Commitments can be abandoned. The only constraint that cannot be overridden is one that is embedded in the architecture of the system itself, operating independently of the intentions of any operator.

The Projects of the 1980s

Margaret Thatcher arrived at Downing Street in May 1979 facing an inflation rate of more than ten per cent and an economy that had been managed, for three decades, on the assumption that the state could spend its way to prosperity. She had read Hayek. She had met Friedman. When she picked up Hayek's The Constitution of Liberty at a Conservative Party meeting and placed it on the table, declaring "this is what we believe," she was not performing a rhetorical gesture. She was identifying the intellectual foundation of a programme that would impose considerable short-term pain in pursuit of a structural change in the architecture of British monetary governance.

The pain was real. The Bank of England's base rate was raised to seventeen per cent in November 1979. Unemployment climbed from 5.7 per cent to more than twelve per cent by 1983. Manufacturing output contracted sharply. Communities built around industries that had survived on the implicit subsidy of inflation and managed exchange rates found the ground cut away from beneath them. The political cost was enormous and sustained. What Thatcher was attempting, and what she largely achieved, was the Volcker programme in British conditions: the deliberate use of monetary contraction to break inflationary expectations, accepting severe short-run costs in exchange for the restoration of price stability.

Reagan's project was pursued in different institutional circumstances but from a compatible intellectual position. The Federal Reserve, under Volcker — appointed by Carter and retained by Reagan — raised the federal funds rate to twenty per cent, triggering the sharpest recession since the 1930s. Inflation, which had reached nearly fifteen per cent in 1980, fell to below four per cent by the mid-decade. The political courage required to hold the monetary contraction through two years of rising unemployment and fierce Congressional opposition was considerable, and it is impossible to understand the success of the Volcker disinflation without acknowledging that Reagan, despite the immediate political costs, provided the political cover that made it possible.

Both projects succeeded in their primary objective. Inflation was broken. The inflationary expectations that had embedded themselves in wage contracts, investment decisions, and the behaviour of financial markets were, over several years of painful adjustment, extinguished. The Great Moderation that followed — two decades of low inflation, stable growth, and declining macroeconomic volatility — was in substantial part the legacy of the monetary discipline imposed in those years.

But both projects also failed, in a deeper and more structural sense that only became visible in retrospect. What Thatcher and Reagan achieved was not the installation of a constraint. It was the demonstration that better operators could produce better outcomes within an unconstrained system. They replaced reckless monetary management with prudent monetary management. They did not change the architecture. The discretionary authority of central banks remained intact. The political incentive structure that had produced the 1970s inflation remained intact. And when the operators changed — when the institutional memory of the Volcker disinflation faded, when the political cost of restraint once again seemed to outweigh the distributed and diffuse cost of expansion — the system reverted to its structural tendency. The Greenspan put, the post-2008 quantitative easing, the pandemic expansion described in Chapter Three: each was the product of an unconstrained system operating according to its own incentive structure. Each was entirely predictable from the architecture. And each was the precise outcome that Hayek and Friedman had diagnosed, half a century earlier, as the inevitable consequence of giving governments the power to create money without limit.

The Gold Standard and Its Virtues

To understand what Bitcoin restores, it is necessary to understand what was lost. The Gold Standard, in its various forms across the nineteenth and early twentieth centuries, was not a perfect monetary system. It was a structural constraint, and like all structural constraints it imposed costs as well as benefits. The costs are well documented: deflationary pressures during periods of gold scarcity, limited capacity for counter-cyclical monetary policy, the vulnerability of peripheral economies whose gold reserves were hostage to the commercial decisions of the dominant financial centres. Critics of the Gold Standard, from Keynes onward, have had no shortage of real deficiencies to point to.

What is less frequently acknowledged is what the Gold Standard was actually doing at a structural level, because that is precisely what its abandonment destroyed. The Gold Standard was a negative feedback loop. It was the balancing mechanism described in Chapter Three: a constraint on monetary expansion that operated independently of the intentions of any government or central bank. When a country's currency was convertible to gold at a fixed rate, the expansion of the money supply was bounded by the physical stock of gold held in reserve. A government that spent beyond its means, financing the excess through monetary expansion, would watch its gold reserves drain as holders of the inflating currency exercised their convertibility right. The drain was visible, measurable, and undeniable. It was a signal that could not be seasonally adjusted, retrospectively revised, or linguistically finessed. A vault that was emptying spoke with a clarity that no monetary policy statement could replicate.

The system had a further virtue that tends to be overlooked in historical assessments. It was depoliticised. The constraint on monetary expansion did not depend on the good intentions of a central bank governor, the independence of a monetary policy committee, or the electoral calculations of a finance minister. It depended on physics. Gold was scarce because geology made it scarce. No quantity of political will could change the rate at which it was mined from the earth. The constraint was external to the system of governance and therefore immune to the system of governance's most persistent pathology: the tendency to subordinate long-term structural discipline to short-term political convenience.

This is what Nixon destroyed in August 1971. He did not merely adjust an exchange rate or modify a policy framework. He removed a structural constraint that had, however imperfectly, anchored monetary expansion to physical reality for the better part of a century. What replaced it was not a superior constraint. It was no constraint at all — only the discretionary authority of institutions whose incentive structure, as Hayek had diagnosed in 1976 and as the subsequent half-century of monetary history has confirmed, consistently favoured expansion over restraint. The measuring instrument of the global economy was severed from its physical anchor and left to float on the judgements and conveniences of those who controlled it. The consequences, as Chapter Three demonstrated in detail, were structural and cumulative. They are still compounding.

The Technological Completion

Bitcoin, viewed through this lens, is not a radical departure from monetary tradition. It is a return to it — one made possible not by geology but by mathematics. To understand this precisely, it is worth holding the parallel directly in view.

The Gold Standard's fundamental virtue was its supply constraint: the quantity of monetary gold was governed by a physical reality that no government could expand by decree. Its fundamental vulnerability was that the constraint was, ultimately, capturable. Governments could confiscate gold — as Roosevelt did with Executive Order 6102 in 1933, requiring American citizens to surrender their gold coins and certificates to the Federal Reserve. They could redefine the peg — as Britain did repeatedly across the nineteenth century when the terms of convertibility became inconvenient. They could suspend convertibility — as every major combatant did at the outbreak of the First World War, and as Nixon did, supposedly temporarily, in 1971. The constraint was real, but it was subject to override by sovereign authority. The tower, in Ferguson's language, could always reach it.

Bitcoin's supply constraint is governed not by geology but by protocol. The twenty-one million unit cap is enforced by the mathematical consensus of a distributed network whose participants span every jurisdiction on earth. There is no vault to raid, no peg to redefine, no convertibility to suspend. A government that wished to increase the supply of Bitcoin would need to persuade the entire global network of Bitcoin nodes to accept a protocol change — an undertaking that is not merely politically difficult but architecturally designed to be so. The distributed nature of the network is not an accident of its development. It is, as Chapter Five described in the context of Ferguson's analysis, a deliberate architectural choice whose purpose is precisely to make the network resistant to capture by any concentrated authority. The tower cannot reach it, because there is no single point of control for the tower to seize.

This is the property that Hayek was reaching for in 1976 but could not build. His proposed competitive currency system required private issuers — banks or commercial institutions — whose currencies would compete on the basis of their value stability. The weakness of the proposal, as critics noted at the time, was that private issuers remained subject to regulatory capture, competitive pressure, and the same incentives toward overissuance that had corrupted government money. The issuer, however well-intentioned, retained discretionary authority over supply. Bitcoin eliminates the issuer. The supply schedule is not a promise made by an institution. It is a feature of the protocol, as unchangeable as the rules of arithmetic. No issuer can renege, because there is no issuer.

Friedman's k-percent rule was an attempt to achieve the same end through institutional commitment: bind the central bank to a rule, publish the commitment, and hold the operators to it. The weakness was identical: commitments can be abandoned, rules can be rewritten, and institutional memory fades. The Federal Reserve's abandonment of money-supply targeting in the early 1980s was not a failure of will by any individual. It was the entirely predictable behaviour of an institution operating within a political system that consistently rewarded expansion and punished restraint. The rule required virtuous operators. Bitcoin requires no operators at all. The constraint is architectural.

Conserving Value

The political conservative's case for Bitcoin is, therefore, not a recent invention. It is the logical conclusion of a tradition that has been building its argument for fifty years. That tradition correctly diagnosed the disease — the inflationary bias of unconstrained monetary systems, the political incentive structure that consistently favours expansion, the slow confiscation of savings that Keynes described and Friedman quantified. It prescribed remedies that were correct in principle but insufficient in practice, because they relied on institutional commitment rather than architectural constraint. Bitcoin is what the tradition was reaching for: a monetary system whose supply cannot be expanded by political decision, whose rules cannot be rewritten by sovereign authority, and whose integrity depends on no single custodian's virtue.

The thermodynamic conservative's case is equally precise, and it maps onto the political case with an exactness that is worth pausing to appreciate. A conservative asset, in Saylor's sense, is one that conserves the economic energy deposited in it. It does not leak. The leakage in a fiat monetary system is the rate of monetary expansion: each new unit of currency created dilutes the purchasing power of every existing unit, transferring real value, invisibly and continuously, from those who hold money to those who create it. An asset that conserves value must be immune to this dilution. It must have a supply that cannot be expanded by the decision of any authority. It must, in other words, be structurally conservative in the political sense simultaneously with being thermodynamically conservative in the engineering sense.

Gold came close. Its supply was constrained by geology and therefore largely immune to political manipulation in the short run. But its constraint was imperfect: new mining production added to the above-ground stock at a rate of one and a half to two per cent per year, a slow but compounding dilution. Its constraint was also capturable in the long run: sovereign authority could and did override it when the political pressure became sufficient. Bitcoin's supply constraint is more absolute than gold's in both respects. The issuance schedule is predetermined to the satoshi, decelerating in a series of programmed halvings until the final coin is mined sometime in the twenty-second century. And it is structurally immune to sovereign capture in a way that physical gold never was, because there is nothing physical to seize.

The conservative case for Bitcoin is therefore not an argument about price appreciation, speculative potential, or technological novelty. It is an argument about architecture. It is the observation that, for the first time in monetary history, there exists an asset whose supply constraint is both mathematically precise and politically uncapturable — an asset that is conservative in both the political and the thermodynamic sense simultaneously, and that does for monetary discipline what Hayek, Friedman, Thatcher, and Reagan were trying to do with institutional tools that proved insufficient to the task.

The tradition did not fail. It was incomplete. The diagnostic was correct: unconstrained monetary systems drift toward expansion, and that expansion constitutes a slow confiscation of the savings of those who cannot protect themselves from it. The remedy was correct in its direction but inadequate in its mechanism: rules, commitments, and institutional arrangements are not constraints in the structural sense. They are policies. And policies, as the System Dynamics analysis of the preceding chapters has demonstrated at length, are no substitute for architecture. Bitcoin is the architecture.

In the next chapter, we return from intellectual history to institutional practice. Having established the structural argument for Bitcoin as both a conservative and a conserving asset, we trace the corporate machine that Saylor built to acquire it — a machine that drew not on operating cash flow but on the capital markets themselves, converting the fiat system's own instruments of expansion into a mechanism for accumulating the fixed-supply alternative. It was, in its way, the most audacious act of monetary judo in corporate history.

Chapter 7

The Alchemy of Structure

"All models are wrong. The practical question is how wrong do they have to be to not be useful."
— John D. Sterman, All Models Are Wrong: Reflections on Becoming a Systems Scientist, 2002

There is a word that recurs, with telling frequency, in accounts of those who have applied System Dynamics rigorously to real problems and been proven right. The word is alchemy. It surfaces in Forrester's own reflections on the reception of *Urban Dynamics*, whose counterintuitive findings struck audiences as something between sorcery and provocation. It surfaces in the reactions of MIT graduate students who have just played the Beer Game and are confronted with the graph of their own oscillating inventory decisions, which they did not predict and cannot immediately explain. And it surfaces, in a different register, in the responses of financial analysts confronted with the structural arguments of those rare capital allocators who appeared to see, years in advance, the consequences of dynamics that everyone else was watching without comprehending.

The word is imprecise but its meaning is clear. Alchemy describes the transformation of base material — apparent complexity, apparent randomness, apparent unpredictability — into something legible and actionable. The alchemist does not possess supernatural insight. He possesses a framework that the uninitiated lack. He sees structure where others see noise, accumulation where others see fluctuation, delayed consequence where others see sudden shock. The transformation is not mystical. It is analytical. But to those operating without the framework, its results are indistinguishable from magic.

This chapter asks two related questions. The first is how Michael Saylor's decision fits into the longer story of monetary evolution and the development of capitalism as a system — not as an isolated corporate event but as an act of structural intelligence applied to the most consequential feedback system in the modern world. The second is why the analytical framework that made that act of structural intelligence possible remains, sixty-five years after its founding, so conspicuously absent from the institutions most directly affected by its insights. The answer to the second question, it turns out, illuminates the first.

An Actor in a Longer Story

The chapters of this book have traced a structural argument across several centuries. The Gold Standard imposed a physical constraint on monetary expansion. Bretton Woods maintained a weakened version of that constraint through the convertibility of the dollar. Nixon's suspension of convertibility in 1971 removed the constraint entirely, converting the global monetary system from a closed-loop control architecture to an open-loop one, with no governor independent of the discretion of the institutions charged with managing it. The consequences — the inflationary 1970s, the Volcker shock, the Great Moderation's illusory stability, the post-2008 expansion, the pandemic acceleration — were structurally predictable from the feedback architecture described in Chapter Three. What each episode had in common was that it appeared, to those watching flows rather than stocks, as a surprise. And what it had in common with the episode before it was that the accumulated imbalance, built during the period of apparent stability, eventually produced a correction of severity proportional to the delay.

Against this backdrop, Saylor's 2020 decision is not best understood as a corporate treasury allocation. It is best understood as an act of structural diagnosis followed by structural response. He looked at the post-1971 monetary system and identified it, correctly, as a system with a dominant reinforcing loop and a disabled balancing constraint — a system structurally configured to erode the real value of stored monetary claims indefinitely. He looked at the available alternatives and identified one whose supply architecture was immune to the feedback dynamics driving the erosion. And he acted, at institutional scale and at personal reputational risk, on the conclusions of the analysis.

What places him in the longer story of monetary evolution is not the audacity of the decision but its structural logic. Capitalism, as a system, has always produced actors who understood its feedback dynamics better than their contemporaries: who saw the accumulation of leverage before the deleveraging crisis, who identified the structural fragility behind the apparent stability, who positioned themselves to benefit from the delayed consequences of imbalances that the consensus was attributing to noise. What is unusual about Saylor is not the quality of his structural insight but his decision to publish it — to explain, at exhausting length and across hundreds of hours of recorded conversation, precisely what he had seen, how he had seen it, and why he had acted on it. Most actors who reach the same conclusions by similar means keep their methods to themselves. Saylor gave the model away. That generosity, whatever its motivation, makes his case uniquely available for examination.

Why the Alchemy Remains Rare

Jay Forrester published *Industrial Dynamics* in 1961. The discipline he founded has been continuously developed, refined, and published for more than six decades. Its software tools are freely available. Its core textbook — Sterman's *Business Dynamics* — is a thousand pages of rigorous, well-illustrated exposition. The System Dynamics Society runs an annual international conference. The field has produced consequential work on climate, epidemiology, supply chains, and economic cycles. And yet the number of practitioners capable of building and interpreting a System Dynamics model of any real complexity remains, in Forrester's own description, vanishingly small relative to the number of organisations and decision-makers who would benefit from one.

When John Sterman delivered the talk that became his 2002 paper All Models Are Wrong: Reflections on Becoming a Systems Scientist — given upon receiving the Jay W. Forrester Award, the field's highest honour — he offered the most candid account of this paradox that the literature contains. The paper's title is its argument: every model is a simplification, every simplification omits something, and the discipline's first requirement is therefore humility about the limits of one's own analysis. But the paper's deeper argument is about what it takes to become the kind of thinker who can use simplified models well. It requires, Sterman writes, the rigorous and disciplined use of scientific inquiry combined with respect and empathy for others and other viewpoints and, most importantly, a genuine willingness to seek evidence that one is wrong. These are not qualities that institutional environments reliably cultivate. They are, in many respects, qualities that institutional environments systematically select against.

The reasons are structural. Sterman's decades of experimental research, encapsulated in the bathtub experiments and the Beer Game analyses described in Chapter One, established that the failure to reason correctly about feedback and accumulation is not a mark of low intelligence or poor education. It is a consequence of the mismatch between the linear mental models that human cognition defaults to and the nonlinear dynamics that govern complex systems. Correcting this mismatch requires not just instruction but repeated experiential learning — the kind that the Beer Game provides, placing people inside a system and showing them the gap between what they intended and what their decisions produced.

This takes time. It requires a tolerance for being wrong. And it produces conclusions that are frequently at odds with the institutional consensus, which means that acting on them requires a willingness to be isolated and ridiculed for years before the delayed feedback signal validates the analysis.

Senge's 2016 memorial for Forrester, written after Forrester's death at the age of ninety-eight, captures something that the academic literature rarely states directly. The quality that made Forrester exceptional, Senge observed, was not his technical mastery — though that was formidable — but his capacity for what Senge called not knowing. Forrester was the professor who regularly prefaced his remarks with the observation that he did not really understand a topic deeply. In a university environment whose currency was certainty, this was disarming to students and alarming to colleagues. But Senge came to understand it as the cognitive prerequisite for the kind of structural analysis that System Dynamics requires. You cannot model a system whose behaviour surprises you if you are not genuinely open to being surprised. The willingness to sit with unresolved complexity, to hold conflicting data without forcing premature synthesis, to update the model when the evidence demands it: these are the marks of the serious systems analyst, and they are the marks of a mind that institutional life rarely nurtures and often punishes.

Sterman's 2018 essay System Dynamics at Sixty, published on the sixtieth anniversary of the field's founding, asks what Forrester would do if he were young today. Its answer is both hopeful and sobering. Hopeful because the computational tools, data availability, and interdisciplinary scope available to a systems analyst today are incomparably richer than anything Forrester had access to when he sketched WORLD1 on a notebook on a flight from Bern. Sobering because the institutional barriers to serious structural analysis remain as formidable as ever: the preference of policymakers and executives for conclusions that confirm existing strategies rather than challenge them, the short time horizons of financial markets, the incentive structures that reward the production of confident point forecasts rather than the honest acknowledgement of structural uncertainty. The alchemy is harder than ever to sell and more valuable than ever to possess.

The Guarded Knowledge Hypothesis

Forrester observed, in the conversation with Senge quoted in Chapter One, that those who truly understood System Dynamics had no particular incentive to popularise it. A tool that reveals counterintuitive structural truths about complex systems is, almost by definition, more valuable to its possessor if others do not possess it. The insight is not new to the history of knowledge: alchemists kept their formulae in cipher; mathematicians published proofs only after their competitive advantage was exhausted; traders guard their models as the most proprietary of assets. What is unusual about System Dynamics is that the formula is entirely public, freely documented, and yet very rarely practised at the level that confers genuine analytical advantage. The barrier to adoption is not secrecy. It is difficulty — the difficulty of acquiring the cognitive habits, the tolerance for complexity, and the willingness to act on counterintuitive conclusions that the discipline requires.

In financial markets, this difficulty functions as a moat. If structural analysis of the kind that SD enables is genuinely more predictive than linear extrapolation of current trends — if it allows the practitioner to see the overshoot before the market does, to identify the stock accumulating behind a delayed feedback signal that the consensus is treating as permanent stability — then the value of that analytical advantage is directly proportional to its scarcity. Publishing the method destroys the advantage. The rational response of those who have crossed the barrier is to use the method, not to explain it. The result is that the most consequential applications of structural systems thinking in financial history are precisely the ones least likely to be documented, attributed, or acknowledged.

This brings the argument to Ray Dalio, and it is worth being precise about what is and is not being claimed. The claim is not that Dalio is a closet practitioner of formal System Dynamics in the Sterman sense — that Bridgewater's investment process runs on Vensim models and causal loop diagrams. There is no published evidence for this and the hypothesis would be implausible in any case. The claim is structural rather than biographical: that Dalio's analytical framework, as documented in his published work and in his famous animated video How the Economic Machine Works, exhibits the essential hallmarks of structural systems thinking, whether he arrived at them through the MIT tradition or through four decades of self-directed empirical learning on his own balance sheet.

The evidence is worth examining. Dalio's economic machine model is, stripped of its accessible presentation, a qualitative stock-and-flow analysis of credit and debt dynamics. It identifies the primary stocks — total credit outstanding, debt levels relative to income, the stock of productive assets — and traces the feedback loops that govern their accumulation and depletion. It distinguishes the short-term debt cycle from the long-term debt cycle in terms that map directly onto the analysis of systems with loops operating at different frequencies. It identifies the critical delayed feedback signal — the point at which accumulated debt service obligations exceed income flows — that triggers the deleveraging dynamic. And it frames the 2008 financial crisis not as an external shock but as the predictable consequence of structural imbalances that had been accumulating for decades, visible to anyone who was watching the stocks rather than the flows.

Dalio's near-catastrophic 1982 prediction — in which he publicly forecast a depression that failed to arrive — is instructive in exactly the way that Sterman's paper on model failure is instructive. The structure of Dalio's analysis was broadly correct: debt had accumulated to levels that historically preceded severe contractions, and the feedback dynamics he had identified were real. What the model got wrong was the delay. His response was not to abandon the structural framework. It was to build uncertainty about delays into the framework itself — to construct portfolios robust to a range of structural scenarios rather than optimised for a single point prediction. This is precisely the epistemological lesson that Sterman's Forrester Award paper teaches: the value of a structural model lies not in its predictive precision but in its ability to clarify the range of outcomes consistent with the system's structure and to identify the feedback signals that would distinguish among them.

The Power of Ideas: When a Book Changes the World

There is a dimension of this story that conventional economics is ill-equipped to capture, and that System Dynamics handles with a naturalness that is one of the discipline's least celebrated virtues. It is the causal power of ideas.

Standard economic models treat agents as operating on information: prices, quantities, incentive structures, constraint sets. The agent responds to what the market tells them, and the model predicts behaviour from that response. What this framework cannot easily accommodate is the phenomenon of an idea that restructures the agent's entire interpretive framework — that does not add a new data point to an existing model but replaces the model entirely. It cannot accommodate, in other words, the kind of event that occurred in May 2020, when Michael Saylor, having spent several weeks working through a reading list that included Saifedean Ammous's *The Bitcoin Standard*, emerged from the exercise and committed his company to purchasing four hundred and twenty-five million dollars of Bitcoin.

Saylor's own account of the sequence is unusually precise. In the foreword he subsequently contributed to a revised edition of Ammous's book, he described the moment of recognition with a directness that few corporate executives bring to the documentation of their intellectual conversions. "It was this book," he wrote, "more than any other, that provided the holistic economic framework that I needed to interpret the macroeconomic forces reshaping our world." The book was, in his formulation, the instrument of diagnosis. It provided the conceptual vocabulary — drawn from the Austrian tradition of Mises and Rothbard — that made the structural analysis of the fiat system legible in monetary terms rather than merely in the engineering and thermodynamic terms that Saylor's MIT background had already supplied. In his public summation of its impact, he was characteristically terse and precise: "I read it and I decided to buy \$425m of bitcoin. The best compliment I can give this book is that it blew my mind."

It is worth pausing on the strangeness of this. A man of fifty-five, with thirty years of operational experience running a technology company, with an MIT education in the most rigorous analytical tradition of the twentieth century, with a personal financial history that included the largest single-day loss of personal fortune ever recorded — this man sat down in the spring of 2020 with a book published two years earlier by an economist most of his peers had never heard of, and the book changed everything. Not incrementally. Not by adding a new variable to an existing model. Entirely. It replaced the model.

The book had been sitting in the world for two years before Saylor found it. It had been read by tens of thousands of people in the Bitcoin community, most of whom already believed what it argued. It had been discussed on podcasts, cited in articles, recommended on forums. None of that reached Saylor. What reached him was the macroeconomic emergency of March 2020 — the pandemic, the lockdowns, the Federal Reserve's announcement of unlimited asset purchases — which created a specific kind of cognitive readiness: the readiness of a man who has spent twenty years building a fortress balance sheet, who is watching in real time as the fortress is being undermined by forces he can see but cannot yet name. The book arrived at the moment of maximum receptivity. It named the forces. And in naming them, it made legible a structural argument that Saylor's own engineering instincts had been circling without resolution.

This is how books have always worked at their most consequential. Not as repositories of information that readers absorb passively, but as catalysts that release a reaction already latent in the reader's mind. Charles Darwin spent twenty years accumulating evidence for natural selection before he encountered Malthus's Essay on Population, and it was Malthus — a book written sixty years earlier about a different subject entirely — that supplied the missing mechanism and crystallised the theory. Martin Luther had been wrestling with the theology of grace and indulgence for years before he nailed his theses to the door at Wittenberg; it was Gutenberg's press, the distribution technology that Gutenberg himself never politicised, that turned a local theological dispute into a civilisational rupture. In each case, the idea was not new. The conditions for its reception were. The book arrived when the world was ready to be changed by it.

Ammous's book arrived in Saylor's hands in May 2020, at a moment when the world was printing money at a rate that made the structural argument for fixed-supply assets not merely intellectually interesting but existentially urgent for anyone responsible for a corporate treasury. The resonance was not between the argument and an abstract principle. It was between the argument and the precise, measurable, daily-compounding problem that Saylor was staring at on his balance sheet. The book did not persuade him of something he had no reason to believe. It resolved a tension that had been building for months, supplied the framework that his engineering mind required to convert unease into analysis and analysis into action, and gave him the language — Austrian, monetary, historical — to articulate what his thermodynamic intuition had already been telling him. When he describes the experience as having his mind blown, he is not using the phrase casually. He is describing the specific cognitive event of a mental model being replaced: the discontinuity, the disorientation, the sudden clarity of seeing something that had previously been invisible, and the irreversibility of having seen it.

The book is a medieval technology. Johannes Gutenberg's press democratised it in the fifteenth century; the Kindle and the global distribution infrastructure of the twenty-first century made it instantaneously available in thirty-seven languages. But its essential nature has not changed. It is still a single mind speaking, at length and in sequence, to another single mind. It cannot be scrolled past. It cannot be summarised by an algorithm into three bullet points. It demands the reader's sustained attention over hours and days, and in demanding that attention it creates the conditions for the kind of deep cognitive restructuring that a paragraph, an article, or a podcast cannot. *The Bitcoin Standard* is not a long book — fewer than three hundred pages in most editions — but it is dense, sequential, and constructed with the deliberate architecture of an argument that must be followed from its foundations. To understand its conclusion, the reader must have worked through its premises. And that work, that sustained intellectual engagement with a single coherent argument, is what produces the framework transformation that Saylor describes. The information is not deposited in a passive mind. The mind is actively rebuilt by the encounter.

Mises published the argument in 1912. Rothbard extended it in 1962. Ammous translated it in 2018. Saylor acted on it in 2020. The chain runs over a century, from a lecture room in Vienna to a corporate boardroom in Virginia, transmitted through the oldest technology of intellectual dissemination that literate civilisation has produced. Standard economic models have no variable for this. They have no way to account for the causal force of a century-long conversation in monetary theory arriving, via a book, in the mind of a single corporate executive at the moment of maximum receptivity. System Dynamics at least has the conceptual vocabulary: the stock of actors who have absorbed a framework, the inflow driven by the availability and accessibility of the literature that carries it, the reinforcing loop that accelerates as those actors make their conclusions public and reduce the activation energy required for the next reader to follow. The book is the inflow mechanism. The idea is the stock. And once the stock is large enough — once enough minds have been rebuilt by the encounter — the behaviour of the system changes.

System Dynamics captures this dynamic with a precision that conventional economics cannot match, precisely because SD treats sentiment, conviction, and the diffusion of ideas as causal factors as real as interest rates or population changes. In a causal loop diagram of the Bitcoin adoption process, the stock of institutional actors with an Austrian-informed monetary framework is a genuine stock, accumulated by an inflow of reading, persuasion, and intellectual conversion, and depleted only by the kind of public humiliation that makes the holder of a heterodox view abandon it. The rate of inflow is governed by the availability of accessible literature, the credibility of those who have already converted, and the macroeconomic conditions that make the argument feel urgent. All three of these inflow drivers were at their historical maximum in 2020. The stock accumulated rapidly. The adoption loop, already operating below the threshold of institutional visibility through the preceding decade of Bitcoin's existence, crossed the threshold that Saylor's purchase marked, and the behaviour of the system shifted. The square, in Ferguson's formulation, proved faster than the tower — and it proved faster because a book had done its work on a single receptive mind at the moment of maximum need.

The Arguments Against

The hypothesis deserves honest scrutiny, because it is not without weaknesses. The most serious objection is epistemological: the claim that SD confers a reliable analytical advantage in financial markets is, at bottom, an empirical one, and the evidence for it is circumstantial rather than controlled. We observe successful capital allocators whose frameworks appear consistent with systems thinking. We observe that their methods are opaque. We infer that the opacity conceals structural analysis of a kind that confers advantage. But this inference is not falsifiable in the conventional sense. The alternative hypothesis — that the same successful allocators are beneficiaries of survivorship bias, leverage, and the secular decline in interest rates that has inflated returns across asset classes for four decades — cannot be easily ruled out from the published record.

A second objection is more fundamental. System Dynamics does not predict the future. It clarifies the structural tendencies of a system — the behavioural modes that its feedback architecture makes possible, the scenarios consistent with its stocks and flows. This is enormously valuable for policy analysis and for understanding what kind of dynamics a system can produce. But financial markets are, in an important sense, reflexive: they incorporate information about structural tendencies into prices, and the act of many participants modelling the same feedback dynamics changes the dynamics themselves. The value of structural insight in financial markets depends in part on its not being widely shared, and the moment it becomes widely shared, its implications are priced in.

These are real objections and they should not be dismissed. What they argue against, however, is not the value of structural systems thinking but the naive version of the alchemy claim: the idea that possessing a systems model guarantees financial success. The more defensible version of the claim is narrower: that structural systems thinking, applied with the humility and epistemic discipline that Sterman's Forrester Award paper describes, provides a more reliable basis for understanding the directional tendencies of complex systems than the linear extrapolation and narrative reasoning that dominate most investment analysis. It does not guarantee right answers. It makes wrong answers less likely and more instructive when they occur.

Saylor and the Test of the Gold

Return, for a final time, to Saylor. In the summer of 2020, he sat in an office in Tysons Corner, Virginia, and worked through an analysis whose conclusions he could not have been confident would be vindicated in his professional lifetime. The feedback dynamics he had identified — the post-1971 monetary architecture's structural tendency toward expansion, the attractor dynamics of a fixed-supply asset in a world of elastic money, the network effects that Andreessen had identified a decade earlier, and the Austrian monetary argument that Ammous had synthesised into a form he could apply directly to his corporate balance sheet — were real and structurally compelling. But the history of structural analysis in financial markets is littered with correct diagnoses that arrived decades early and destroyed the careers of those who acted on them before the feedback signal manifested.

What Saylor had that many earlier structural analysts lacked was an institutional position that transformed the delay problem. A corporate treasury does not face a margin call. It does not have redemption gates. It does not report to investors who will withdraw capital at the first adverse quarterly mark. The decision to convert MicroStrategy's reserves to Bitcoin was not a leveraged bet with a time horizon determined by the patience of counterparties. It was a structural commitment by a self-funding enterprise to a long-run directional thesis. If the feedback signal took five years to arrive rather than one, the company would survive. If it took ten years, it would survive that too. The only scenario in which the thesis was irreversible was the one in which Bitcoin's protocol itself failed — which would have required a breakdown of the distributed consensus mechanism that the network's entire architecture was designed to prevent.

This is the structural elegance of the decision that commentary fixated on its volatility consistently missed. Saylor was not playing a game with a short time horizon against sophisticated counterparties with access to the same information. He was making a structural commitment to a directional dynamic whose logic he had modelled rigorously and whose architecture he understood to be, in the relevant respects, immune to the reflexivity problem that undermines structural analysis in most liquid markets. Bitcoin's supply could not be expanded because everyone agreed it would be expanded. The consensus of the network enforced the supply constraint independently of what any investor believed about it.

What the alchemist's test requires is not that the formula be kept secret but that the gold be real. Saylor gave the formula away. He published the analysis, explained the framework, hosted conferences for corporate treasurers, gave hundreds of hours of interviews in which he traced the structural argument from first principles to its conclusions. The gold — the structural validity of the analysis — was either real or it was not. If it was not, the transparency of the method would expose it. If it was, the transparency would accelerate the network adoption dynamics that the analysis predicted.

Structure Determines Behaviour, Always

Forrester's foundational proposition — the sentence that opens Chapter One of this book — is not a claim about simplicity. The systems that exhibit the most consequential structural dynamics are often the most superficially complex: monetary systems, biological networks, technological adoption curves, the long-run dynamics of capitalism itself. The proposition is that beneath the apparent complexity lies a feedback architecture whose properties can be identified, whose behavioural modes can be characterised, and whose implications can be traced even when the timing of their manifestation cannot be predicted with precision.

This proposition has been publicly available since 1961. Its tools are free. Its textbooks are in print. And yet the number of organisations, institutions, and capital allocators that have absorbed it at the level of genuine structural competence remains, by any reasonable estimate, a small fraction of those who would benefit from doing so. This is not a failure of System Dynamics. It is a confirmation of one of its central insights. The same policy resistance that Forrester identified in urban dynamics, the same institutional inertia that prevented the *Limits to Growth*'s structural findings from reshaping economic policy, the same preference for linear extrapolation over feedback analysis that Sterman has demonstrated experimentally: these are not aberrations. They are the structural features of institutions and cognitive systems that have been optimised for performance in stable environments and that fail, consistently and predictably, when the environment is governed by nonlinear dynamics.

The financial establishment that dismissed Saylor's 2020 decision as reckless was not making an error of intelligence. It was making a structural error: the error of evaluating a long-run architectural commitment using the mental models appropriate to short-run price speculation. It was watching the flow — the volatility of Bitcoin's price in any given quarter — and missing the stock: the long-run structural dynamics of a monetary system without a governor, and the equally structural dynamics of a fixed-supply network attracting capital from that system. It was confusing the flow for the system.

And yet the idea that corrected that error — the Austrian monetary argument, transmitted through a century of scholarship from Mises to Rothbard to Ammous and arriving at Saylor's desk in the spring of 2020 in the form of a book — had been available to any reader who sought it out. The alchemy was not hidden. It was simply difficult, counterintuitive, and at odds with the institutional consensus. In the end, that is the most important thing the story of System Dynamics and the story of the Bitcoin Standard have in common. Both are bodies of knowledge whose implications are available to anyone willing to do the work of understanding them. Both have been largely ignored by the institutions most directly affected by their insights. And in both cases, the actors who did the work, absorbed the implications, and acted on them with the patience that structural analysis requires — rather than the urgency that flow-watching demands — appear, to those who did not do the work, to have performed something very close to alchemy.

The gold, in Saylor's case, will be tested by time and by the further unfolding of the structural dynamics that this book has traced. The structure of those dynamics does not change because the testing takes longer than expected. Delays are not refutations. They are features of complex systems, and they are, as every serious practitioner of System Dynamics learns eventually, the most consequential features of all.

* * *

In the Epilogue, we step back from the argument and ask what it means — for the institutions of money, for the future of capitalism, and for those who must navigate a world in which the structural dynamics traced in these pages are still, quietly and relentlessly, compounding.

Epilogue

The Tide Comes In

"Everything's quarterly driven, people are either euphoric or freaking out. And actually, you've got to take a longer view."
— Kwasi Kwarteng, former Chancellor of the Exchequer, 2026

In the spring of 2025, approximately five years after Michael Saylor converted MicroStrategy's treasury reserves into Bitcoin and invited the world to dismiss him, sixty-one publicly listed companies held Bitcoin on their corporate balance sheets. Their collective holdings stood at eight hundred and forty-eight thousand coins — four per cent of the entire Bitcoin supply. The number had grown by thirty-one per cent in 2024 alone, and in the first two months of 2025 it nearly doubled again. Corporate treasuries were acquiring Bitcoin at a rate that consistently outpaced the exchange-traded funds whose January 2024 approval by the Securities and Exchange Commission had been greeted as the decisive moment of institutional legitimation. The decisive moment, it turned out, had been August 2020.

This book has been an argument about structure. Its claim has been that the behaviour of complex systems — monetary systems in particular — is determined by their feedback architecture rather than by the intentions of their operators, and that the most important dynamics in such systems are often the least visible: the stocks accumulating behind delayed feedback signals, the balancing loops progressively disabled, the reinforcing loops operating below the threshold of institutional attention until the moment they cross it. The data of 2024 and 2025 is not the proof of that argument. Proofs are not available in the social sciences, and delays are not refutations. But it is the feedback signal arriving. It is the structure doing what the structure was always going to do.

The Three Clocks

It is worth pausing, before we follow the argument to its contemporary manifestations, to register the timescales involved. The book has traced three separate intellectual traditions converging on a single structural conclusion, and each operates on its own clock.

The longest is the Austrian clock. Ludwig von Mises published *The Theory of Money and Credit* in Vienna in 1912. He diagnosed, with a precision that the mainstream economics of his day rejected and the events of the following century confirmed, the structural tendency of credit expansion to produce business cycles, and the structural tendency of fiat money to erode the purchasing power of those who held it. Murray Rothbard extended the framework in 1962. Saifedean Ammous translated it into the digital age in 2018. Michael Saylor read it in the spring of 2020 and spent four hundred and twenty-five million dollars. The clock ran for a hundred and eight years before it struck the hour.

The second is the System Dynamics clock. Jay Forrester sketched WORLD1 on a notebook on a flight from Bern in 1970 and spent the rest of his ninety-eight years building and defending a discipline that could model the feedback structures of complex systems with a rigour that conventional linear analysis could not match. His intellectual heir John Sterman spent thirty years demonstrating, experimentally and with characteristic humility, that the failure to reason correctly about stocks and flows is not a mark of stupidity but a structural feature of human cognition — and that correcting it requires not instruction but experiential encounter with systems that behave in ways one did not predict. The discipline Forrester founded in 1961 found its most spectacular financial application in 2020, in the decisions of a man who had absorbed its core principles as an MIT undergraduate in 1987. The clock ran for thirty-three years.

The third is the Bitcoin clock. Satoshi Nakamoto published the white paper in October 2008, in the ruins of the financial system whose structural fragility Chapter Three of this book has traced in detail. The timing was not accidental. The white paper's opening sentence — a proposal for a peer-to-peer electronic cash system requiring no trusted third party — was a direct response to the tower's most spectacular modern failure. The network launched in January 2009. By August 2020, when Saylor made his first purchase, it had been operating continuously for eleven years, accumulating nodes, establishing trust, compounding adoption, and waiting for the institutional threshold that his decision would help it cross. The clock ran for eleven years.

Three clocks. Three intellectual traditions. Three timescales. Converging, in the spring and summer of 2020, on a corporate office in Tysons Corner, Virginia, where an MIT-trained engineer with a systems analysis background was sitting on half a billion dollars of melting cash and reading a book. The convergence has the structure of inevitability in retrospect. It did not feel that way to anyone watching it happen.

The Adoption Wave

What followed Saylor's decision has the character, in System Dynamics terms, of a reinforcing loop crossing a threshold. Below the threshold, the loop's output is too small to attract institutional attention. The signal is present, but the noise is louder. Above the threshold, the signal dominates. Each new institutional actor who enters the network increases its legitimacy, reduces the activation energy required for the next actor, and strengthens the network effects that Andreessen had identified a decade earlier. The adoption curve, which had been growing quietly for years, inflected.

The inflection produced a secondary wave of corporate imitators whose relationship to the original thesis varies considerably. At one end of the spectrum are companies that have absorbed the structural argument — that the post-1971 monetary architecture is structurally configured to erode the purchasing power of fiat reserves, and that Bitcoin's fixed supply makes it structurally immune to that erosion. At the other end are companies that have absorbed the price chart and the fear of missing out. One analyst, surveying the landscape of 2025 corporate Bitcoin adopters, put the distinction with characteristic bluntness: the clearest missteps came from companies that "panicked" or reversed course, revealing no long-term view. The biggest mistake of the year, he observed, was not volatility — it was inconsistency.

This distinction matters structurally. A company that holds Bitcoin because it has diagnosed the feedback architecture of the fiat monetary system and concluded that a fixed-supply asset is the rational response to that architecture will hold through volatility, because the volatility does not invalidate the diagnosis. A company that holds Bitcoin because the price went up and its CFO was nervous about looking behind the curve will sell at the first significant drawdown, because the holding was never grounded in structural analysis. The former is a long-run position. The latter is a momentum trade with a Bitcoin label. The adoption wave of 2024 and 2025 contains both, in proportions that will only become clear when the next severe correction arrives and we observe who holds and who folds.

Bernstein Private Wealth Management projected in 2025 that public companies globally could allocate as much as three hundred and thirty billion dollars to Bitcoin over the following five years. Standard Chartered anticipated that corporate treasury adoption would be the primary driver of Bitcoin's largest-ever dollar rally. Whether these projections prove accurate is, from the structural perspective this book has taken, a secondary question. The primary question is whether the actors driving the adoption have understood the argument or merely the price. The structure will eventually distinguish between them.

Kwarteng and the Irony of the Tower

No single episode in the recent history of Bitcoin's institutional adoption is more structurally revealing — or more saturated with historical irony — than the emergence, in the early months of 2026, of Stack BTC: a London-listed company whose executive chairman is Kwasi Kwarteng, former Chancellor of the Exchequer.

Kwarteng occupied the office of Chancellor for thirty-eight days in the autumn of 2022. During that period he co-authored, with Prime Minister Liz Truss, a fiscal package that became known as the mini-budget: the largest proposed programme of unfunded tax cuts in modern British history, financed by over seventy billion pounds of additional borrowing. The market's response was immediate and categorical. Sterling fell to a thirty-seven-year low against the dollar. Gilt yields spiked to levels that threatened the solvency of pension funds operating liability-driven investment strategies. The Bank of England was forced into emergency bond purchases to prevent a systemic collapse. Kwarteng was dismissed after thirty-eight days. Truss followed shortly after. The episode remains the most vivid recent demonstration in British political memory of what happens when a government attempts to spend beyond the means that its monetary architecture can credibly support — of what happens, in other words, when the tower overreaches.

By the spring of 2026, Kwarteng had become executive chairman of a company whose explicit purpose is to accumulate Bitcoin as a treasury reserve, on the thesis that fiat currencies are structurally unreliable stores of value. The structural irony is almost architectural in its neatness. The man who participated in the most spectacular modern demonstration of the fiat system's fragility — who watched from the inside as the market's feedback signal dismantled his government in a matter of days — has drawn the conclusion that a monetary system governed by political discretion is not one in which surplus value can be safely stored. He has, in other words, learned from the feedback. Whether he has drawn the right lesson for the right reasons is a question for his biographers. But the structural logic of his trajectory is coherent.

In a recent interview with CoinDesk, Kwarteng was candid about both the failures of his brief tenure and the broader fiscal position he believes the UK now inhabits. He warned that the country is trapped in a doom loop: "You're spending more money than you can raise in taxation," and rising taxes ultimately "kill incentives in the economy." He critiqued the short-termism that he sees as endemic to both political and financial cultures: "Everything's quarterly driven, people are either euphoric or freaking out. And actually, you've got to take a longer view." On Bitcoin, his formulation was direct: "Bitcoin is entering its institutional phase and this is a real opportunity." And in a corporate video that repays attention, he articulated the underlying structural argument with a precision that would have been unthinkable in a serving finance minister: "A Bitcoin treasury company is accumulating Bitcoin because it is a far greater preserver of wealth than a fiat currency."

Stack BTC, as of early 2026, holds thirty-one Bitcoin — a sum that would not register against MicroStrategy's six hundred thousand. It is a small company on a small exchange, and it is early. But its significance is not its current holdings. Its significance is what it represents in the longer structural argument: the feedback signal reaching the political class. When a former Chancellor of the Exchequer, having watched a fiat monetary system deliver its most vivid recent verdict on undisciplined government spending, responds by building a vehicle to accumulate the fixed-supply alternative, the argument has travelled a very long way from a white paper published to a cryptography mailing list in 2008.

The arrival of Nigel Farage as a shareholder — with a six per cent stake acquired at five pence per share in March 2026 — adds a further political dimension that requires careful handling. Farage has been among the most prominent British advocates for Bitcoin in the political mainstream, pledging to establish a Bitcoin reserve within the Bank of England and to allow tax payments in cryptocurrency if Reform UK were to take power. His alignment with Kwarteng's venture is politically legible: two figures from the political right, both critical of the existing monetary and fiscal architecture, positioning themselves around an asset whose entire design philosophy is a structural critique of that architecture. Labour's response — questioning why Farage was investing with "the architect of Liz Truss's disastrous mini-budget" — missed the structural point entirely, as political responses to structurally grounded arguments frequently do.

Forrester's Unfinished Work

Jay Forrester never modelled the monetary system directly. He modelled factories and supply chains, cities and ecosystems, and finally the entire world — but the feedback architecture of the post-1971 monetary order, the system whose consequences this book has traced across seven chapters, was not among the formal models his group produced. He identified the removal of the gold constraint in 1971 as a structural change of first-order importance — Senge recalls him observing that it had transformed the monetary system from a closed-loop to an open-loop architecture — but he did not pursue the analysis.

This book has been, in one reading, an attempt to complete that line of inquiry: to ask what the System Dynamics framework, applied to the post-1971 monetary architecture, would reveal about the structural tendencies of that system and the rational responses available to actors who understood them. The answer, traced through the chapters of this book, is that the system exhibits exactly the behaviour that a control engineer would predict of any open-loop system: persistent drift in the direction of least resistance, periodic crises when accumulated imbalances can no longer be concealed, and a structural incapacity for self-correction that is not a failure of the system but a feature of its design. Bitcoin is not the discovery of this structural tendency. It is an engineering response to it. And the

Satoshi Strategy — the decision to convert a corporate treasury from the instrument of that drift into the fixed-supply alternative — is the most fully articulated institutional expression of that response yet produced.

Forrester lived to ninety-eight, long enough to see the Bitcoin network established and growing, but he died in November 2016, before the institutional adoption wave he might have recognised as a structural threshold. One imagines the conversation he might have had with Sterman about it: the feedback loops, the delays, the stocks and flows. One imagines his response to the argument of this book. Whether he would have found it persuasive is, of course, unknowable. What can be said is that the analytical framework is his. The conclusions it leads to, applied to the monetary domain he never quite reached, are the natural extension of an intellectual tradition he spent sixty years building and defending.

What Remains Uncertain

The most honest epilogues acknowledge what they cannot resolve, and this one is no exception. The structural argument for Bitcoin as a stable attractor in a world of monetary expansion is, this book has argued, compelling. But compelling arguments about structural tendencies are not predictions about outcomes, and the distance between a structural tendency and its realisation can be very long indeed.

The tower's resources are not exhausted. Governments can regulate, restrict, and raise the cost of accessing the Bitcoin network in ways that fall short of the architectural capture that the protocol is designed to resist. They can create CBDC alternatives and mandate their use for taxation and public services. They can apply capital gains treatment to every Bitcoin transaction, creating friction that slows adoption without ending it. They can coordinate internationally in ways that fragment the network's jurisdiction-spanning properties. None of these responses can expand the supply of Bitcoin. None can override the protocol. But they can slow the reinforcing loop of adoption, extend the delays, and make the attractor state harder to reach on any given timeline. The tower cannot capture the square. It can, however, make the square expensive to enter.

There is also the question of whether the adoption wave currently underway is structurally sound or structurally fragile. A corporate treasury that holds Bitcoin because its CFO has diagnosed the feedback architecture of the fiat monetary system is a structurally stable participant in the adoption loop. A corporate treasury that holds Bitcoin because its CFO was afraid of missing the next rally is a source of volatility that, at sufficient scale, could produce the kind of forced selling that temporarily validates the sceptics and discourages the next cohort of adopters. The adoption wave of 2024 and 2025 is large enough, and diverse enough in its motivations, that the fragile component is real. How large it is, and when it will be tested, are questions the structural analysis cannot answer.

What the structural analysis can say is this: the feedback architecture of the post-1971 monetary system has not changed. The reinforcing loop — expansion, asset inflation, further expansion — continues to operate. The ratchet continues to turn. The purchasing power of fiat reserves continues to erode at whatever rate the monetary authorities' current policy choices imply. These dynamics do not pause while the adoption wave consolidates, or while regulators deliberate, or while sceptics compose their objections. They are structural. They are continuous. And they are, as every episode in this book's account of the post-1971 monetary order has confirmed, indifferent to the institutional consensus about whether Bitcoin is a legitimate response to them.

The View from the Square

This book began with a cattle ranch in Nebraska and a boy who built a wind-driven electrical system from old automobile parts because the ranch had no power and he understood, in the wordless way that practical engineers understand things, that the problem had a structural solution. It has traced the intellectual tradition that boy created, through vacuum tubes and servomechanisms and SAGE and the Beer Game and the bathtub experiment, to the point where that tradition intersects with the most consequential monetary development of the twenty-first century.

Along the way it has argued that Michael Saylor's 2020 treasury decision was not the act of a speculator or an evangelist, though he has performed both roles with considerable energy. It was the act of an engineer who had been trained to see feedback structures, who looked at the monetary system through that lens, and who drew the conclusion that the structure of the system made a specific outcome not merely possible but structurally probable: that capital would migrate from a monetary instrument without a governor to one with a governor that no authority could override. He then acted on the conclusion with the decisiveness that the analysis warranted and the patience that the delay structure required.

The feedback signal is now arriving. Sixty-one public companies. Eight hundred and forty-eight thousand coins. A former Chancellor of the Exchequer building a Bitcoin treasury on the Aquis Stock Exchange. A US Strategic Bitcoin Reserve established by executive order in March 2025. BlackRock's Bitcoin ETF reaching fifty billion dollars in assets under management faster than any ETF in history. These are not predictions. They are data points from 2025 and early 2026. They are the system behaving as its structure suggests it should, on a timeline that no model could have specified but that the structural analysis made intelligible.

Kwarteng's observation that everything is quarterly driven — that people are either euphoric or panicking, and that the necessary corrective is to take a longer view — is, whether he knows it or not, the most concise restatement of the System Dynamics ethos that any politician has recently produced. It is also, coming from the man whose thirty-eight-day tenure as Chancellor ended in the most public demonstration of the fiat system's fragility that British political memory contains, a statement that carries a particular weight. The tower taught him what it could not teach itself: that short-termism, in monetary policy as in corporate governance, produces exactly the structural consequences that a properly calibrated feedback model would have predicted.

Forrester's proposition — structure determines behaviour — does not require advocates. It requires only that the structure be examined and the behaviour observed. The structure of the post-1971 monetary system has been examined in these pages, at some length and with, it is hoped, the rigour that Sterman's discipline demands. The behaviour has been observed across five decades of accumulating consequence. What remains is for the reader to draw their own conclusions — about the analysis, about Bitcoin, about the institutions of money, and about the kind of knowledge that makes the difference between watching a system and understanding it.

The tide, as Sterman might say, does not pause to consult the consensus. It comes in.

* * *

The author wishes to acknowledge the intellectual debts this book has accumulated. To Jay Forrester, who built the framework. To John Sterman, who refined it and defended it. To Peter Senge, who made its human dimensions legible. To Saifedean Ammous, whose synthesis of three intellectual traditions into a single accessible argument catalysed the events this book describes. And to Michael Saylor, who gave the model away.

Index

distributed resilience, *Chapter 1*

E

exchange-traded funds (ETFs), Bitcoin, *Chapter 3, Epilogue*

F

Federal Reserve, *Introduction, Chapter 1, Chapter 2, Chapter 3, Chapter 4, Chapter 6, Chapter 7, Epilogue*
feedback loop, *Introduction, Chapter 1, Chapter 2, Chapter 3, Chapter 5, Chapter 6, Chapter 7, Epilogue*
Ferguson, Niall, *Introduction, Chapter 5, Chapter 6, Chapter 7*
fiat currency, *Introduction, Chapter 3, Chapter 4, Chapter 6, Chapter 7, Epilogue*
Fifth Discipline, The (Senge), *Chapter 1*
Forrester, Jay Wright, *Introduction, Chapter 1, Chapter 2, Chapter 4, Chapter 7, Epilogue*
Friedman, Milton, *Chapter 6*

G

gold standard, *Introduction, Chapter 3, Chapter 6, Chapter 7*
gold window, *Introduction, Chapter 3*
Great Moderation, *Chapter 3, Chapter 6, Chapter 7*

H

Hayek, Friedrich, *Chapter 6*
Human Action (Mises), *Chapter 1*

I

Industrial Dynamics (Forrester), *Chapter 1, Chapter 2, Chapter 7*

K

Keynes, John Maynard, *Chapter 3, Chapter 6*
Kwarteng, Kwasi, *Epilogue*

L